Anyone *Can* Knit

Anyone *Can* Knit

A STEP-BY-STEP GUIDE TO ESSENTIAL KNITTING SKILLS

ARCTURUS

This edition published in 2014 by Arcturus Publishing Limited
26/27 Bickels Yard, 151–153 Bermondsey Street,
London SE1 3HA

ISBN: 978-1-78404-048-2
AD004065UK

Printed in China

CONTENTS

INTRODUCTION

In its most basic form, knitting is a very simple craft and its development through the past few decades has depended upon its accessibility to almost anyone. In earlier centuries its position in society has fluctuated from a well-respected craft producing high-demand luxury items to a low demand folk craft and back again. In the Victorian period it was adopted as a 'parlour art' but by the 1930s it had become more a functional craft.

Knitting fell out of favour between the 1960s and 1990s in the wake of the popularity of man-made fibers, the development of industrial knitting machines, and a general lack of interest in the 'handmade'. As knitting became less popular, knitting patterns and good yarns became less widely available.

Towards the end of the 1990s, however, people started questioning the merits of mass production and the handmade item came back into fashion. The global recession of 2008 and onwards boosted this. Knitting shops sprung up around the world, workshops were advertised, and a generation that had dismissed the skills of their mothers or grandmothers, started to pick up sticks and create. What's more, they demanded good quality yarns made from natural fibers prompting a revival in natural fibers that even reached the Yorkshire mills in England and continues today.

This recent revival means that knitting currently flourishes as both luxurious and mundane, as form and function. The craft has been explored to its extremes, from knitting with 6ft long giant sized needles and plastic bags to delicate knitted wedding dresses. Knitting can be used to express and appreciate both the absurd and the exquisite. Equally adaptable to the domestic and the industrial arena, requiring draftsman skills and mathematical calculations, as well as artistic flair and fashion sense, it is both an art and a science. Knitting has become as ubiquitous as the humble sheep. You may not be aware of just how many everyday objects are, or can be, knitted because familiar objects are not always consciously noticed for what they are. By taking up the art of hand knitting yourself, you will learn to appreciate and understand the everyday knitted objects in your world, as well as gain pleasure from creating your own.

The joy of the finished object is not the only motivator for learning to knit, hand knitting is a therapeutic craft, and the process is thought to have many health benefits, including keeping the mind strong and active, promoting healthy joints, and helping to reduce stress.

Knitting is also appealing because it doesn't require a big financial investment to get started, results are quickly achieved and it is portable. Once you have mastered the basics, knitting can be done while watching TV, listening to the radio and travelling on the bus or train. Taking knitting to a higher level, where you can tackle complex patterns and designs, will take time and practice but this should not put you off because the rewards of knitting a simple object are often just as great. The simplicity of good design, combined with some simple skills, make this a hobby that anyone can try, and succeed in.

OVERVIEW

How to use this book

This book will guide you through the very first steps of hand knitting, from casting on your first stitches and creating simple objects through to making accessories, items for the home and garments. The speed at which you work through the book will depend on your temperament, the time you can make available to learn and practice, and how quickly you pick up the techniques. You may decide you want to master every technique one at a time or that you want to dip in and out of different sections. However, because the book is progressive, you should bear in mind that projects in the later sections may require skills taught earlier. Each tutorial section is followed by a pattern or two using the techniques learnt. However, you should also look for other patterns to work through at each level to help you practice more, www.Raverly.com is a great resource for this, or visit your local yarn shop where you will be given expert advice. Finishing Techniques (pages 60-66) is a key section of the book that you will need to refer to all the way through from your first project to the most complex garment in the book. At the back of the book (pages 120-7) there are hints and tips that you will also find useful throughout, particularly for correcting mistakes.

Getting Started

Just buy a few essentials to get started but choose the best quality materials you can afford. It is disheartening to learn a new skill with poor materials. The absolute basics you need are: a quantity of yarn, a pair of sharpened sticks (known as 'needles'), a pair of scissors, a darning needle with a large eye and blunt end, and a tape measure.

When you choose your very first set of materials, be aware that your choice of yarn and project will determine the choice of needles. You need to know how the yarn behaves when it is worked to decide which needles you will need and whether the yarn is right for your project. This is hard to do by just looking at or feeling the yarn but, don't worry, almost all yarns have a 'ball band' or label attached which contains information such as recommended needle size and what fibers are in the yarn. Buying your first materials in a specialist knitting shop rather than online is a good idea because you can ask for expert advice.

Your first purchase as a knitter

NEEDLES

The recommended yarn for the first project in this book is Libby Summers Chunky and for this you will need a pair of size 8mm [US size 11] needles. If you decide to start with another project, read the materials section of the pattern to see what size of needles you will need.

The table below provides the US and UK needle sizes used with different 'weights' (thicknesses) of yarn.

UK Needle Size	Metric Needle Size	US Needle Size	Type of Yarn
14	2mm	0	Lace, Fingering
13	2.25mm	1	Lace, Fingering
12	2.75mm	2	Lace, Fingering
11	3mm	-	Lace, Fingering
10	3.25mm	3	4ply, Sport, Baby
-	3.5mm	4	4ply, Sport, Baby
9	3.75mm	5	Double Knit, Light Worsted
8	4mm	6	Double Knit, Light Worsted
7	4.5mm	7	Double Knit, Aran, Worsted, Afghan
6	5mm	8	Aran, Worsted, Afghan
5	5.5mm	9	Aran, Worsted, Afghan
4	6mm	10	Chunky
3	6.5mm	10½	Chunky
2	7mm	-	Chunky
1	7.5mm	-	Chunky, Craft, Rug
0	8mm	11	Chunky, Craft, Rug
0	9mm	13	Super Chunky, Bulky, Roving
0	10mm	15	Super Chunky, Bulky, Roving
-	12mm	17	Super Chunky, Bulky, Roving
-	16mm	19	Super Super Chunky
-	19mm	35	Super Super Chunky
-	25mm	50	Super Super Chunky

Once you have decided what size of needles to buy, you have a choice of material. Wooden needles, such as birch or rosewood, tend to be more expensive and the harder the wood, the more expensive again. Bamboo needles can bend over time but are an economical choice and are nice to work with. Plastic or metal needles tend to be the cheapest but are not so nice to hold. Metal needles can irritate the skin and plastic needles can be slippery. If you have stiff yarn that is difficult to work, plastic needles can help but for most yarns a basic bamboo or birch needle is a good beginner's choice. You may wish to consider buying a set of needles with a pair in each size as this is often more economical than buying individual pairs. However, if you discover you like knitting with one particular thickness of yarn, you may never use the rest of the set. Also, you will not know yet if you prefer using circular or straight needles.

Circular, straight and double pointed needles

There are three different types of needles available. Straight needles are rigid pins of varying length and are for traditional seamed knitting. A circular needle has rigid points on each end of a flexible 'cord' or 'cable', which means you have one needle that acts as two straight ones. As you knit you pass the stitches from one rigid point to the other and then allow them to slide round the wire as you work. You can use circular needles to work back and forth in rows in the same way as straight needles or you can continue to work round and round in a circle to create a tube of knitting. Circular needles were originally designed for creating tubular objects such as hats but they are becoming more popular as a needle of choice for any project, particularly given that they are easy to carry around.

Double pointed needles are bought in sets of four or five, and are used all at once for creating small tubes of knitting, such as socks, or fingers on gloves. Sock knitting tends to be a specialist area of its own, and is beyond the scope of this book. You are unlikely to need double pointed needles in the short term.

To make your decisions easier, start with a pair of 25cm long straight bamboo needles. They are the easiest to begin with and will always be useful.

Other needles and bits and bobs

You may have seen some very short needles, often with a bent centre. These are cable needles, and are used for holding two or more stitches at the front or back of your work while you work other stitches around them. This technique of cabling essentially twists your work to create texture, depth and pattern. One small diameter and larger diameter cable needle is a useful addition to your knitting bag but you are unlikely to be using them straightaway.

Other equipment that you might wish to add to your knitting bag as you progress is listed over the page. Don't worry if you don't know what these are for at the moment. Their use will be explained as you work through the book.

EQUIPMENT

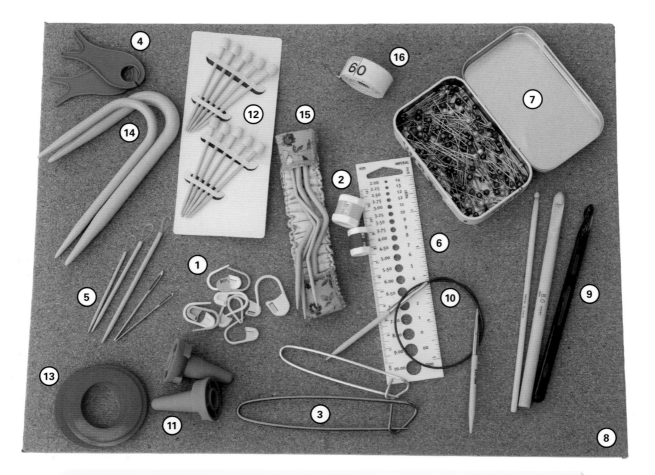

Equipment list

1. Stitch markers – for marking the position of a certain point in your work
2. Row counters – for helping you to count your rows
3. Stitch holders – for holding a number of stitches not being worked on
4. Bobbins – for colourwork
5. Specialist darning needles – for sewing up different thicknesses of yarn
6. Needle gauge – for checking needle sizes
7. Box of pearl or glass headed long length pins – for pinning your knitting together when blocking and sewing up
8. Blocking board or pin board [as shown]
9. Crochet hooks – for picking up stitches
10. Circular needles – for knitting in the round
11. Needle tip protectors – for keeping needles safe
12. Bamboo pins – for holding sections of knitting together when sewing up
13. Pompom makers
14. Large cable needles – for use with super chunky yarn
15. Standard cable needles – used to temporarily hold the stitches in place
16. Tape measure
17. Fine mist sprayer for blocking [not photographed]

YARN

The characteristics of different yarns

We have already noted that the characteristics of the yarn will affect the size of the needles. The characteristics of the yarn depend on the fiber used, the thickness and how the yarn is spun.

You might assume that yarn is simply fiber of different sorts combined in different ways. However, air is just as significant as fiber because it provides more volume than fiber in most spun yarns. A yarn where all the fibers are parallel and straight is called a 'singles' yarn. Most often though, fibers are twisted together to create a yarn that is strong enough to knit with. Highly twisted yarn is known as 'lively' and tends to untwist or snarl. Low twist yarns produce a soft fabric, but can be weak. The number of components of a twisted yarn are described by 'ply', so if two separate strands are twisted together to make a yarn it is called '2 ply' and if 8 are used, it is called '8 ply'. Most commercial yarns are plied yarns although there are some singles yarns available on the market (such as Libby Summers' Chunky) but they are rare because it is difficult to produce a singles yarn strong enough to knit with. Hand spinners will often produce good singles yarns, but in small quantities for a specialist market.

Some countries use the ply of yarn as a shorthand for its thickness, but this is misleading because a yarn with two plies can be thicker than a yarn with eight.

Yarn composition

The composition of a yarn is an important factor in defining its character and its use. There is a huge range of materials that can be turned into yarn, but broadly speaking they can be divided into three categories – natural fibers, man-made fibers and mixed fibers. There is currently a revival in the appreciation of natural fibers and consequently a huge range of different yarns to choose from. As a general guide, a yarn made from natural fibers will have elasticity, warmth and breathability and sometimes be softer than a man-made fiber. Unless treated, it will shrink if washed at high temperatures making it only suitable for dry cleaning or hand washing. Some natural fibers will pill or ball.

Man-made fibers have the advantage of being machine washable but they do not feel as nice and are not usually as warm. They may be unsuitable for some types of garments due to a lack of elasticity. Mixed fibers may be machine washable.

It is helpful to decide on what you are going to make before purchasing your yarn or to choose a project that is suitable for yarn you have already bought.

It is important to read the 'ball band', or yarn label, which will have information about the composition of the yarn and washing instructions. However, it will not tell you about other characteristics such as whether the yarn will stretch with wear or pill. For this you need a general knowledge of the properties of different materials so you can make your own assessment. The table on following page should help you.

Fiber	Source	To wear	Absorbency	Handle	Drape	Durability
Alpaca	alpacas	warm	high	soft or coarse	good	good
Angora	angora rabbits	warm, soft and light	very low	soft or coarse and light	good mixed with other fibers	poor
Bamboo	bamboo plant	warm in, winter cool in summer	high	very soft	good	odour resistant, UV resistant
Cashmere	cashmere goats	very warm	high	soft	good	fair, tends to pill
Cotton	cotton plant	cool	high	soft	good	good
Linen	flax plant	fresh, cool	high	stiff	good	good
Mohair	angora goats	warm in winter, cool in summer	low	soft and light	good	very good
Silk	silkworm	warm in winter, cool in summer	high	smooth and soft	very good	very good
Wool	sheep	warm	high	soft or coarse	good	fair

Care	Other	Typical use
can shrink, should be dry cleaned	breathable, repels rains, creases drop out, elastic, lanolin free, hypoallergenic	hot water bottle covers, bedding, blankets, cowls, scarves, jumpers
dry clean	halo (fluffiness), little elasticity, felts easily	luxury sweaters, undergarments and sportswear
usually machine washable	hypoallergenic	blankets, baby garments, summer clothes
dry clean	warmest yarn in the world	sweaters, scarves and undergarments
easy care	creases	summery garments, children's wear
easy care	creases	summery garments, home accessories
dry clean	high lustre & sheen, naturally elastic, does not felt, difficult to tear	jumpers, outdoor clothing, blankets
usually machine washable	holds dye well, but also odor	shirts, jackets, ties, formal wear, luxury accessories
can shrink, should be dry cleaned creases drop out, elastic	breathable, repels rains	jumpers, hats, scarves

Choosing and substituting yarns

There are two different approaches to buying yarn. You may see a yarn you love, buy it for its own sake and then choose a pattern to match the yarn. The alternative is to choose a pattern first which will determine the yarn you select. It is recommended to use the same yarn stated in the pattern. Choosing a different yarn is a risky business, even if you pick one that supposedly works up to the same 'tension' as the yarn in the pattern. Even a slight change in the thickness of the yarn can make a substantial difference to the amount of yarn needed. A change in yarn will alter the overall appearance of the finished item and it may not be useable.

Remember too that yarn affects the character of stitch patterns, and the designer will have spent time and thought matching the stitch pattern to the yarn to produce a certain effect. Smooth and solid coloured yarns will give high stitch definition, so will be suitable for a complex stitch pattern. Boucle, multi coloured or tweedy yarns will give less definition and some stitch patterns will be lost to the eye in all the texture that is created by the yarn.

THE LANGUAGE OF KNITTING

As a novice embarking on your knitting journey, you might be surprised to discover that you need to learn a new language as well as a new skill. This may excite you or terrify you in equal measure, but it is not as difficult as it sounds because all good patterns will translate knitting terms into plain English for you in an 'Abbreviations' section. There may also be a 'Notes' section if any of the techniques described are unusual or complex.

This section aims to demystify the language of knitting and equip you with the skills to interpret abbreviations and terms as they crop up on your knitting journey. It will also be a good reference point for you to return to over time.

Tension [Gauge]

You might have heard knitters talking about 'tension' or 'gauge'. In knitting, the term 'tension' means almost the opposite of the dictionary definition of 'the state of being stretched tight'. You are aiming for a piece of fabric which is neither too tight nor too loose for your purpose. The US term of 'gauge' is more fitting, being defined as 'the thickness, size, or capacity of something, especially as a standard measure'.

Your gauge or tension in knitting is calculated by measuring your work to see how many stitches you used or rows you knitted to achieve 10cm [4in] of knitted fabric. For example, if you knitted in stocking stitch (knit one side, purl the other) and measured a 10cm [4in] square of the knitted fabric and found that you had knitted 22 sts horizontally and 28 rows vertically, this would be your tension. If working from a knitting pattern, it is important that your tension matches the one listed in the pattern. It is recommended that you experiment with knitting small squares of just over 10cm [4in] (13cm [5in] is ideal) until your tension matches that of the pattern (see page 33).

As a beginner it is easier for you to practise and adjust your technique to knit neither too loosely nor too tightly. Too tight or loose a style of knitting will cause you potential difficulties, not only with matching tension but also physical problems, aches and pains and so on. The tutorials will help you develop a good technique, which is neither tight or loose. It is better to practice your technique until you have achieved an average tension, rather than settle for a technique that will mean you will always have to adapt a pattern to fit your non-standard tension.

Pattern Instructions

Most knitting patterns are written with the assumption that the reader is a reasonably competent knitter who understands the basic stitches and techniques. To the uninitiated, patterns can seem incomprehensible but in reality all the complex techniques are simply variations of the basic knit and purl stitch. Once you have mastered the basics – casting on, knit, purl and casting off – you will find that everything else can be worked out from these. The more confusing and sometimes exasperating thing about knitting patterns is that there are many different writing styles, in some cases different abbreviations for the same thing, and different conventions. You may find that you gravitate towards certain designers, yarn companies and magazines because you prefer their style or conventions.

The table opposite and over the page give common knitting pattern abbreviations.

Abbreviation	Definition and explanation
k	knit; with your yarn at the back, insert ndl into front of loop, pointing it towards the back, yarn round ndl, bring yarn through and off.
p	purl; with your yarn at the front, insert ndl into front of loop, pointing it upwards in front of your work, yarn round ndl, bring yarn through and off.
g	gram(mes).
cm[in]	centimetre(s)[inch(es)].
st(s)	stitches; these are the loops on your needle.
RS/WS	right side of work/wrong side of work; ie. the sides that will be seen (RS), or not seen (WS).
st st	stocking stitch [stockinette stitch]; k on RS rows and p on WS rows to create a smooth appearance. Sometimes the purl side is the RS and the knit side is the WS. It is then called reverse st st.
k/p2tog	k/p 2 sts together; ie. insert needle into two loops at once instead of one, and k or p in usual way.
k/pfb	k/p into front and back of next st, thus creating an extra st; k or p in usual way leaving the st on the needle after bringing the yarn through, work into back of st, slip the st off the LH ndl.
beg	begin/beginning; in the context of either measuring your knitting (e.g. meas from the beg, or the beg of.....) or in the context of an instruction telling you which row to start with (e.g. beg with Row 2...)
cont to [work even]	continue/continuing; usually in the context of an established pattern, this instruction will tell you carry on doing what you've been doing (e.g. st st) but may be followed by the instruction 'while also...' and give you something else to do at the same time which you will incorporate into your pattern (e.g. inc or dec) The American term 'work even' means the same thing.
dec	decrease/decreasing; usually appears in a descriptive sentence rather than a row instruction, where the method of decreasing selected either does not matter, or is given elsewhere as the defined method for the pattern. It is usually used where the pattern requires you to decrease as a one off (e.g. 'at end of last row') or create a pattern of decreasing over several rows, such as for an armhole or neckline. Decreasing results in one or more fewer stitch(es).
inc	increase/increasing; as above for decreasing, with reversed shaping. Increasing results one or more extra stitch(es).
foll(s)	follows/following; usually found before a set pattern (e.g. 'as folls...') or before instructions about an impending increase or decrease over a number of rows (e.g. inc in same way on every foll alt row).
alt	alternate; usually refers to a instruction that needs to be carried out every other row, ie. not every single row, but on the first, third and fifth, for example.(e.g. 'inc on next and every foll alt row until....').
meas	measures/measuring; requires you to get your tape measure out and measure your work. The instructions will specify whether you are to measure a section or the whole of your work.
ndl(s)	needle(s); the sharpened stick(s) you are working with.
cn	cable needle; the short double pointed ndl mostly used to create twists in your work
tbl	work into back loop of stitch instead of front loop

Abbreviation	Definition and explanation
patt	pattern; an instruction to work in either a stitch pattern with a set of repeatable row instructions, or embedded in a row (e.g. 'Row 1: Patt 28, M1, patt to end' – in this context, complete the sts around the instruction in the set pattern).
rep	repeat; refers to either some instructions in brackets or between asterisks (*), or refers to set of rows forming a stitch pattern. This should be clear from the context.
rem	remain/remaining; refers to the st(s) left on your ndl after carrying out a dec or inc section. The abbreviation will occur as part of an instruction which will tell you what to do with the st(s) (e.g. 'Rejoin yarn to rem sts..' OR 'Place rem sts on a holder').
yf	yarn forward; normally occurs after a k st, when you need the yarn to be at front of work for the next st, either to p or k that st and create an extra st in front of it. This will cause a hole in your knitting, and is used in lace knitting or where a buttonhole or eyelet is required. If increasing the number of sts, you can knit the next st normally, but if wanting to create a hole without increasing, the instruction will be followed by a dec instruction, such as k2tog or skpo.
M1	make one stitch; this is usually done by picking up the loop between the nearest st on your RH ndl and the nearest st on your LH ndl. If you pull the two sts apart slightly, you will see this horizontal loop appear. Pick this loop up with your RH ndl and place it on your LH ndl. It is now a st for you to work into, but you will need to work into the back of it, otherwise your completed st will face the wrong way and will be a little 'holey'. Insert ndl into the back of the loop, yarn round ndl, through and off in usual way. You will now have one extra st, which looks like it has 'grown' beautifully between the two sts previously mentioned. It is the neatest way of increasing.
yrn	yarn round needle; normally occurs before a p st when you need to create another st before it in order to create a hole, either in lace knitting or a buttonhole or eyelet. If increasing the number of sts, you can purl the next st normally, but if wanting to create a hole without increasing, the instruction will be followed by a dec instruction, such as p2tog. With yarn at front, wrap it round needle going over the needle and underneath it.
yo	yarn over; this instruction is often used interchangeably with yon and yrn, but is actually a different movement from yrn. Yarn over usually occurs after a purl stitch and before a knit stitch, or after a knit stitch before another knit stitch.
yon	yarn over needle; This means the same as yo.
[ ]	work instructions in brackets as many times as directed.
( )	work instructions within parentheses as many times as directed OR used to indicate number of stitches or rows to be worked for different sizes.
**	used as a marker in the pattern for reference, e.g. 'Work from * to **'.
*	followed by ; this usually means repeat the instructions after the asterisk.
sl 1 k/sl 1 p	slip one st knitwise/slip one stitch purlwise. ie. move st from LH ndl to RH ndl without working into it.
yb	yarn back; It is not specified that you should take the yarn back (yb) between knit and purl stitches, unless you would not normally do so to work the next stitch.
kb	Knit back OR knit below; a confusing abbreviation because it has been used to mean both things, which are entirely different. If knit back then simply insert ndl into back of stitch loop instead of front. If knit below then insert ndl into loop from row below instead of the current stitch on LH ndl.

KNITTING TERMS AND TIPS ON PATTERN READING

Reading a knitting pattern can feel like reading Greek to start with but don't worry, you will pick it up as you go along. As well as abbreviations, there are lots of terms used in knitting patterns which are specific to knitting but are not abbreviated. These terms are actually used to help the knitter and with experience you will be able to interpret them correctly.

Common terms are given below, with their definitions.

At the same time: This is written when you need to carry out more than one instruction simultaneously, for example, when shaping the neck and decreasing a raglan sleeve. One set of instructions should be carried out at one end of the row and the other at the other end. The pattern will indicate which end for which instruction

Cast on [CO]: Create a series of loops called stitches, on one of your needles which will be worked to expand your knitting vertically, and sometimes horizontally.

Cast off [Bind Off]: Removing the stitches from the needle whilst simultaneously securing them.

Continue pattern as set [Maintain pattern as established]: This wording usually accompanies another instruction requiring you to work the edge stitches differently from the main pattern (e.g. increasing or decreasing), but you should do so with as little disruption to the pattern as possible, so working the centre stitches in the pattern already set.

Right Front/Left Front: refers to the right front/left front as you are wearing it, not as you are looking at it.

Round: The equivalent of row for circular knitting. You will need a stitch marker to show where each round begins and ends because the stitches are worked continuously without turning.

Row: A row is a series of instructions which should be carried out on the collection of stitches which you have on your needle, after casting on, or after the previous row instructions. After working these stitches, you should turn your work around and then work back the other way, following the next set of instructions. The number of stitches may vary between rows, depending on the previous row instructions, but the 'row count' (ie. the number of stitches you should have after working the row) will be given at the end of the row. If the row count does not change from row to row, no stitch count is provided. Check the number of stitches you have at the end of every row, because if you do not have the right number, you cannot continue in the pattern.

Positive ease: This is a term reserved for garments, and refers to the difference between the actual chest size and the finished measurements of the garment. So for example, a jumper measuring 43cm [17in] from side to side would have 5cm [2in] positive ease for a 81cm [32in] chest.

Work same as left or right piece reversing shaping: This is difficult for a beginner, so the patterns in this book mostly have the instructions for both sides of a garment written out. However, when you tackle other knitting patterns, you will often find this instruction as a short cut. For example, if the pattern gives you the instructions for the left armhole, the decrease will be made at the beginning of a right side row. For the right armhole, the decrease needs to be made at the beginning of the wrong side row. This is fairly simple to translate, but where you are carrying out two sets of instructions at the same time, such as for the neck on a cardigan and a raglan sleeve, it is more complex, particularly if the pattern requires a left leaning or right leaning decrease, then you need to use the opposite technique for the other side of work. (See page 41–3).

STARTING TO KNIT

Casting on

There are many different methods for casting on. The one you choose is usually determined by either the decorative effect desired or practical need. However, a beginner need only start with one or two common, versatile methods.

Creating a Slip Knot

Step 1

Make a slip knot. Start by crossing the short end of yarn over the long end as shown, with the short end on the right.

Step 2

Push the short end through the loop as shown.

Step 3

Holding both long and short end between your fingertips, pull them gently to create a knot at the base of the loop. Adjust the size of the loop by pulling one end only.

Step 4

Put slip knot on one needle, and pull both lengths of yarn gently but firmly so that loop adjusts to the size of the needle. This becomes your first 'stitch' and this needle will be held in your left hand (LH).

Right Hand Thumb method

This is one of the easiest methods of casting on, and is done with just one needle. The new stitches are created with your right hand, by twisting the yarn between your fingers to create a new loop. This method of casting on creates a loose and slightly decorative edge, which is appropriate for garter stitch patterns, or knit and purl patterns. The thumb method is easier to master, but take care when knitting your first row not to knit too loosely, as the cast on edge can look 'loopy'.

Step 1

To create your next stitch, first cross over the long length of yarn attached to the ball, holding the loop created between your fingers and thumb. Hold the first stitch (on the needle) at the base of the stitch between the fingers and thumb of your left hand.

Step 2

Twist the yarn twice at the base of loop, holding the top of the loop with your right hand thumb to ensure the twist stays in place.

Step 3

Slip the loop onto your needle, ensuring that the yarn remains twisted as you do so. Continue to hold the first stitch at the base of the stitch between the fingers and thumb of your left hand and keep the tension in the yarn as you place the stitch on the needle.

Step 4

Pull the yarn attached to the ball to bring the second stitch close to the first and adjust the tension to create an even stitch. Repeat steps 1–4 for each stitch until you have the desired number of stitches on your needle.

Cable Cast On

The cable method is preferred for stocking stitch patterns where a firm and discrete edge is most appropriate or a firm yet elastic foundation is required. The technique is similar to, but easier than the knit stitch, so once you have mastered this technique, you will find the knit stitch relatively straightforward.

Start by creating a slip knot as shown on page 18, following steps 1–4.

Step 1

Insert your right hand (RH) needle behind the stitch on your left hand (LH) needle, ensuring the long length of yarn attached to the ball is on the RH side, and holding the short length of yarn firmly between your left thumb and index finger. This stops the stitch from moving while you work it.

Step 2

Take the long length of yarn between the index and middle finger of your RH, ready to bring it under the needle and over the top of it, whilst continuing to hold the short length of yarn between your left thumb and index finger.

Step 3

Once you have wrapped the yarn around the RH needle, make sure you are holding it firmly between your index and middle finger before moving to Step 4.

Step 4

Bring the new loop of yarn on the RH needle to the front by pushing the point of the RH needle with your LH index finger until the needle pops out on the other side, with the yarn still firmly wrapped around it.

Step 5

Release the tension on the yarn held between your RH index and middle finger to stretch the new stitch and pull it towards the tip of your LH needle, holding the first stitch back with your LH index finger as you do so, otherwise this stitch will travel to the tip of the needle and might fall off.

Step 6

Once you have placed the new stitch on the LH needle, pull the yarn gently to make the loop smaller again so it is the same size as your previous stitch, snug against the needle with a little air pocket.

Step 7

You have now created your second stitch. Repeat steps 1–6 inserting your needle behind the second stitch and in front of the first stitch. This feels more comfortable and is easier to control than the first stitch. Repeat until you have the correct number of stitches.

HOW TO KNIT

The English (or throw) method of the working knit stitch

The knit stitch is the most fundamental knitting technique. Many garments can be created with only the knit stitch, casting on and casting off. If knitting in the round, stocking stitch – the most common smooth stitch used in knitwear – can be created with only the knit stitch. Many other knitting stitches are variations of the knit stitch so once you have mastered it you are well on your way to success. Here is the knit stitch in four simple steps. Work Steps 1–4 for every stitch on your needle. When you have done this, you will have completed a row.

Step 1: IN.

Hold the needle with stitches on in your left hand and the RH needle between index finger and thumb. Insert the RH needle into the loop of the stitch (st) nearest to the point of the LH needle, with tip pointing under the LH needle and straight ahead. Hold the yarn attached to the ball between your fingers as you do so.

Step 2: ROUND.

Pick up yarn with your right hand and wrap it around your RH needle, passing under the needle first before coming over the top. Hold the yarn firmly but not tightly against your needle to secure the action.

Step 3: THROUGH.

Bring the RH needle out of the loop you inserted it into in Step 1 by pushing it towards you with the tip of your LH index finger and bringing it upwards as the tip of the needle peeks through the loop. While you are doing this, the yarn must stay wrapped around the needle so it is drawn through to create the new loop on the RH needle shown in this photo. The original stitch remains on the LH needle.

Step 4: OFF.

Slip the loop worked (not the new loop) off the LH needle. The new loop will now appear on the RH needle as a stitch in its own right.

The knit stitch explained

Here are another set of photos, showing steps 1–4 on a stitch that is in the middle of the row, and with no hands in the photo. Going through the steps again will help you understand the appearance of the row once a few stitches have been worked, as well as seeing some finer details of the movements involved. You will see that the stitch is less 'loopy' than the first one. Some people slip the first stitch of every row for this reason. This can make sewing up more difficult (in my view), and it is preferable to practise achieving a firm edge stitch.

Step 1: IN.
Notice that the yarn is at a lower level than the LH needle and held against the RH needle.

Step 2: ROUND.
Notice that the yarn is temporarily released from being held against the RH needle as it is wrapped around the stitch. Always go under and then over the needle.

Step 3: THROUGH.
You will see that the stitch worked is not loopy this time, and it is easier to bring the needle through without the yarn slipping away than it is with the first stitch in a row.

Step 4: OFF.
The ease of this action is affected by the position of the stitches on the left hand needle. To start with you will be making conscious movements to push them up or down the length of your needle to get them in the right position for working the stitch. With practice this movement will become subconscious and also more efficient. Note the tension in the fabric as it is stretched to ease the stitch off the LH needle. If this tension is too great, your stitches will start to lose their shape, and your hands will get sweaty with the effort.

The continental (or picking) method of working a knit stitch

There is no way of telling whether a knitter has used the 'English' (the knit stitch explained in the previous pages) or 'continental' method by looking at the finished item because the result is the same. The difference in technique is really just about which hand and fingers carry out particular actions. Continental knitting is more movement efficient and so proficient continental knitters tend to be able to knit more quickly than English knitters. Choose the technique that feels most natural to you. Left-handers might prefer continental knitting. The knit stitch is easy, but the purl stitch is harder and there are lots of different methods for it. The continental purl stitch is not taught in this book, but there are many tutorials online.

Step 1: POSITION YARN.
Wrap yarn around your left hand as shown to help control tension.

Step 2: IN AND ROUND.
With RS facing, and yarn held between the index and middle finger of the left hand, insert RH needle into the front loop of the st nearest to the point of LH needle, pointing tip under the LH needle and straight ahead. Grab the yarn with your RH needle, so that it passes under the needle first before coming over the top. Hold the yarn firmly but not tightly to secure the action.

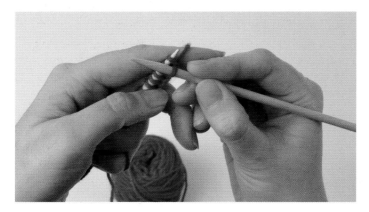

Step 3: THROUGH.
Bring the RH needle out of the loop you inserted it into in Step 2 by pulling it towards you and bringing it upwards as the tip of the needle peeks through the loop drawing the yarn with it. The LH index finger doesn't get involved in this action, as it is holding the yarn in place.

Step 4: OFF.
Slip the loop worked (not the new loop) off the LH needle by tugging with your right hand. The new loop will appear on the RH needle as a stitch in its own right.

Turning your work

When you start a row of stitches, they are on your LH needles with the point facing to your right. Once you have worked the row, the stitches are on the RH needle with the point facing towards the left, as in this photo.

To turn your work, pass the RH needle into your LH, turning it so that the point is now facing to your right. Pass the needle with no stitches on into your RH. You have now reversed the needles, and can begin knitting your next row.

Casting Off [Binding Off]

Casting off is a technique to create a selvedge, simultaneously securing your stitches and stopping any further knitting. If you wish to add to your fabric after casting off, you can re-create the loops by 'picking up' stitches along either the cast off selvedge or one of your other selvedges (see page 65). Sometimes casting off occurs over just a few stitches, when creating an armhole, or buttonhole for example. There are different methods for casting off, the choice based on the decorative effect desired or practical need.

Don't fret about making a mistake while casting off. The most likely result of any mistake is that one or more stitches will need unravelling. Just tug the yarn gently (the end attached to your ball), and the stitch should come undone. Be careful not to pull too hard or you may undo more than one row. If you have managed to tie a knot that doesn't respond to gentle tugging, or your stitch has dropped to the previous row, then you may need to unravel back to the previous row. See page 122 for more tips on correcting mistakes.

A common error is to make the cast-off stitches too tight or too loose – usually too tight. Take a look at the photograph of the finished cast off row (steps 5–6), and try and copy the 'look'. If the air pocket between your stitch and the needle is too big, your cast off edge will be baggy, if it is too small, your knitting will be pulled in at the top spoiling the shape of your work. It is important that your tension is even across the cast off row. Some people always swap to a bigger needle to cast off to avoid making it too tight. I would experiment before taking this step to see how your cast off turns out. Once you have cast off, you are ready to sew up your seams and then you have completed your knitting.

Here is the most common method of casting off.

Step 1:
Knit 2 sts in the usual way.

Step 2:
Take hold of the 1st knitted stitch with your LH needle and pass it over the 2nd knitted stitch, making sure the 2nd stitch stays on the RH needle.

Step 3:
You now only have one st on your RH needle. K another stitch.

Step 4:
Repeat the action of passing the first st over the 2nd. Repeat Steps 3 and 4 until you have 1 st left.

Step 5:
Enlarge the last stitch and cut the yarn leaving a tail. (Read the pattern carefully because there may be instructions on how long to leave the end).

Step 6:
Thread the cut end through the stitch and pull gently until the stitch is the same size as the other cast off stitches.

Joining in a New Ball of Yarn

It might seem obvious to an experienced knitter, but when a new knitter gets to the end of their first ball of yarn, and needs to join in a new one, this can be a cause of great concern. To join in a new ball of yarn, use the technique described on page 50 for changing colour.

The process is exactly the same but your new yarn will be the same colour as your current yarn. It is easier to see this in the two colour version, which is why this is tackled in the colour section. The important principle is that you must not attach your new ball of yarn to the old ball of yarn in any way. Many knitters, even experienced ones, join the yarn with a knot. This will causes problems when you sew up and when you wear your garment. Your new ball should come into operation independently from the old ball of yarn. Always join a new ball at the beginning of a row, which means making a

judgement about when your current yarn is going to run out. As a rule of thumb, you need at least three times in yarn length the width of the stitches on your needle. So if your stitches take up 25cm [10in] of your needle, then you need 75cm [29½in] of yarn to work that row. Knowing this will save unravelling lots of stitches when you run out of yarn halfway through a row. Never be tempted to join a ball in the middle of a row. Always undo the row if you find you have run out. See page 122 for details of how to undo a row.

Garter Stitch

So now you can cast on and do the knit stitch, you can knit something using the most common and basic of all stitches, which is called garter stitch. Garter stitch uses only one technique – the knit stitch. Luckily, it is an attractive stitch and can be used in many different contexts to create beautiful knitting.

If you see the words 'garter stitch' in a pattern, it just means knit every row.

Garter stitch in progress in 4ply baby alpaca/silk mix yarn. Both sides will look the same, so you can choose your 'right side'. Usually this is the side you start with and if so you will be able to recognize when the right side of your work is facing you because the short end of yarn will be on the left hand side of your work (as pictured).

Garter stitch worked in pure wool chunky weight yarn using 8mm[US size 11] needles. There is no discernible difference between the two sides, other than at the cast on edge. A close up of the other side of the work would look exactly the same.

PROJECT 1: WINDSOR

Simple Coffee Set

This delightful coffee set can be quickly knitted up in either two colours or one colour in this gorgeous chunky yarn. There is almost no sewing up and no blocking or pressing so it is an ideal project for a complete beginner. Instructions for changing colour are given on page 50.

Materials

Yarn

COMPLETE SET

One colour version

3 x 50g balls Libby Summers Chunky shade 860 Clear Skies (or substitute for colour of your choice)

Two colour version

2 x 50g balls Libby Summers Chunky shade 100 Elderflower Cream (MC) (or substitute for colour of your choice)

2 x 50g balls shade 500 Yana (CC)

CAFETIERE COVER ONLY

One colour version

1 x 50g ball Libby Summers Chunky shade 860 Clear Skies

Two colour version

1 x 50g ball Libby Summers Chunky shade 100 Elderflower Cream (MC)

1 x 50g ball Libby Summers Chunky shade 500 Yana (CC)

MUG WARMER ONLY

One colour version

1 x 50g ball Libby Summers Chunky shade 860 Clear Skies

Two colour version

1 x 50g ball Libby Summers Chunky shade 100 Elderflower Cream (MC)

1 x 50g ball Libby Summers Chunky shade 500 Yana (CC)

PLACEMAT ONLY

One colour version

1 x 50g ball Libby Summers Chunky shade 860 Clear Skies

Two colour version

1 x 50g ball Libby Summers Chunky shade 100 Elderflower Cream (MC)

1 x 50g ball Libby Summers Chunky shade 500 Yana (CC)

How to make

CAFETIERE COVER INSTRUCTIONS

One colour version

Cast on 20 sts using Libby Summers Chunky shade 860 Clear Skies and 8mm [US11] ndls.
Work in Garter Stitch (ie knit every row) until work meas 28cm [11in].
Cast [bind] off.

TENSION

11 sts and 20 rows to 10cm [4in] square, measured over Garter Stitch Pattern using 8mm [US11] ndls.

To knit a tension square for this project, cast on 16 sts using 8mm [US11] ndls and work in Garter Stitch Pattern until work measures 12cm [4¾in]. Cast [bind] off then measure it. (See page 33 for more details.)

Finished Measurements

CAFETIERE COVER (WHEN SEWN UP AND LAID FLAT)

14cm [5½in] wide
17cm [6¾in] high

MUG WARMER (WHEN SEWN UP AND LAID FLAT)

14cm [5½in] wide
8cm [3¼in] high

PLACEMAT

26cm [10¼in] wide
20cm [8in] long

Abbreviations

See chart on page 127 for specific abbreviations.

Two colour version

Work as for one colour version, changing from MC to CC after 10cm [4in].

Making Up

You do not need to block your work for this design, as it is all knitted in the same stitch, and you do not want to flatten or alter the appearance of the Garter Stitch pattern.

Simply turn your work around 90 degrees, so that the cast on and cast [bind] off edges are vertical, *fold your work in half so that the cast on and cast [bind] off edges meet and the right sides are together (wrong side will be facing you). All you need to do now is sew the top 0.5cm [⅛in] together using a over stitch (see page 64) and then repeat this with the bottom 0.5cm [⅛in]

leaving the entire section in between open. This open section is for the handle of the cafetiere.

MUG WARMER INSTRUCTIONS

One colour version

Cast on 10 sts using Libby Summers Chunky shade 860 Clear Skies and 8mm [US11] ndls.

Work in Garter Stitch (ie knit every row) until work meas 28cm [11in]. You can adapt this to fit the circumference of your mug. Take a flexible tape measure and measure the circumference of your mug to find the measurement that you will need for your knitting. Cast [bind] off.

Two colour version

Work as for one colour version, changing from MC to CC after 10cm [4in].

POCKET

One colour version

Cast on 8 sts using Libby Summers Chunky shade 860 Clear Skies and 8mm [US11] ndls.

Work in Garter Stitch (ie knit every row) until work meas 4.5cm [1¾in].

Two colour version

Work as for one colour version, using CC instead of MC.

Making Up

Before you begin sewing up, turn your work around 90 degrees, so that the cast on and cast [bind] off edges are vertical. Position pocket 2cm [¾in] in from left edge of mug warmer and 1.5cm [½in] up from the bottom. Pin the bottom and sides in place and sew onto the mug warmer using mattress stitch, leaving top edge open.

Make up the rest of the mug warmer as for Cafetiere Cover from *.

PLACEMAT INSTRUCTIONS

One colour version

Cast on 30 sts using Libby Summers Chunky shade 860 Clear Skies and 8mm [US11] ndls.

Work in Garter Stitch (ie knit every row) until work meas 20cm [8in].

Cast [bind] off.

Two colour version

Work as for one colour version, changing from MC to CC after 7cm [2¾in].

Sew in yarn from cast on and cast off edge.

BASICS 1: COMMON STITCHES AND ESSENTIAL TECHNIQUES

The English method of working the purl stitch

The purl stitch is often worked on the wrong side of the fabric, and is the reverse of the knit stitch. When worked continuously on every row, the fabric will have a similar appearance to garter stitch. It can be worked on right side rows, alternating with the knit stitch in various ways to give various textured patterns and effects. There is almost limitless scope for using the knit and purl stitch to complement each other in this way. We will explore this later, but for now, here are the four steps to purl.

Step 1: IN AND UP.
With RS facing and yarn to the right, insert RH needle into the front loop of the stitch nearest to the point of LH needle, pointing tip to the left and up rather than to the right and down.

Step 2: ROUND.
Pick up yarn with your right hand and wrap it around your RH needle, passing over and under the needle first from the right before coming round to the left. Hold the yarn firmly but not tightly against your needle to secure the action.

Step 3: THROUGH.
Bring the RH needle out of the loop you inserted it into in Step 1 by pushing it towards your RH little finger with the thumb of your LH and bringing it upwards as the tip of the needle appears through the loop at the back of work. While you are doing this, the yarn must stay wrapped around the needle so it is pulled through to create the new stitch.

Step 4: OFF.
Slip the loop worked (not the new loop) off the LH needle, using the index finger of your left hand to coax it off, if need be. The new loop will now appear on the RH needle as a stitch in its own right.

Stocking [Stockinette] Stitch

Stocking stitch is probably the most common stitch of all. It has a smooth appearance on the right side, even texture, and high definition. It is therefore the stitch of choice for showing off a yarn's qualities and in particular, for knitting using more than one colour. It is, for example, the only stitch used in Fair Isle knitting and the most common stitch used for stripes and other colourwork.

Stocking Stitch

Row 1 (RS): Knit.
Row 2: Purl.
Rep Rows 1–2.

Working on the knit side – the right side of work.

Working on the purl side – the wrong side of work.

Stocking stitch worked in a pure wool DK on 4mm [US6] needles.

Stocking stitch worked in a multi coloured silk/alpaca mix yarn on 4mm [US6] needles.

Rib

The rib stitch is made up of alternating columns of knit and purl stitches. It is an extremely elastic stitch, and so is very common for cuffs, hems and necklines. It can also be used on its own where a reversible or thick fabric is needed. It is often used alongside other patterns for decorative purposes.

The most common rib is single rib (k1, p1) and is easy to learn as it consists of a simple repeating pattern. The main thing to remember is to move the yarn before or after each stitch is worked. The yarn needs to be back for the knit stitch and forward for the purl stitch. If working with an even number of stitches, the k1, p1 pattern is the same on both sides. If working with an odd number of stitches, you will end with the same stitch you started with and so the pattern will be reversed on the other side, requiring an extra row of instructions. Double rib is created by doubling the number of stitches in each column (k2, p2) and treble rib by trebling the number of stitches in each column (k3, p3).

Note

When an instruction appears in brackets followed by "rep" you should repeat the sequence of stitches inside the brackets for the amount of stitches or portion of row indicated.

Rib pattern, where an even number of stitches is cast on.
Row 1 (RS): (K1, p1) rep to end.
Rep row 1.

Rib pattern, where an odd number of stitches is cast on.
Row 1 (RS): (K1, p1) rep to last st, k1.
Row 2: (P1, k1) rep to last st, p1.

Rib Tutorial

Step 1
Knit one stitch, yarn forward

Step 2
Purl one stitch, yarn back
Repeat steps 1–2 across the row.

Knitting a Tension [Gauge] Square

As soon as you have mastered the very basics of casting on [binding on], casting off [binding off] and the knit and purl stitch, you will probably be itching to knit something you can actually use. If you are knitting something that needs to be a particular size or fit, it is recommended that you check your tension [gauge] before you start your actual project.

Using the same needles and yarn as the pattern you are working from, cast on about 8 stitches more than your pattern says is equivalent to 10cm [4in], and work in stocking [stockinette] stitch (or the stitch recommended in the pattern) for 12cm [4¾in]. Lay this swatch out smoothly and mark off a 10cm [4in] square with pins. Count the number of rows and stitches in between the pins. See page 121 for tips on measuring and counting stitches.

If the number of stitches and rows in your square are the same as the tension [gauge] given in the pattern, then your tension [gauge] is good. If they are not the the same, the usual recommendation for achieving the tension [gauge] in the pattern is to change your needle size and practise working with different needles until you achieve the right tension [gauge]. If there are too many stitches or rows in 10cm [4in], it is recommended that you rework the swatch with larger needles, and vice versa if there are too few stitches. The problem with this advice is that changing the needle size might affect either your stitch count or your row count but not both. I would recommend

that, if you are a beginner and can bear to do this, then practise your technique until you achieve the right tension [gauge], rather than changing your tools. Practice really does pay off, but only perfect practice makes perfect knitting!

PROJECT 2: CARLOTTA

Simple Wrist warmers

Wrist warmers are increasingly popular for busy people constantly on the go. This is a lovely project for a near beginner who wants to practise their knit and purl stitches and get a fantastic accessory into the bargain. For complete beginners, knit the one colour version using standard cast on and cast off techniques. Once you have practiced colour knitting and rib cast [bind] off, you can return to this project and knit the two colour version, using rib cast [bind] off to refine the edge.

Materials

Plain Version
2 x 50g balls Libby Summers Fine Aran (photographed in 890 Sunset Sky and 101 Coastal Cream)
Pair 4mm [US6] ndls
Pair 5mm [US8] ndls

Two colour Version
1 x 50g ball Libby Summers Fine Aran shade 874 Vintage Green (Yarn A)
1 x 25g ball Libby Summers Fine Aran shade 890 Sunset Sky (Yarn B)
Pair 4mm [US6] ndls
Pair 5mm [US8] ndls

TENSION

18 sts and 40 rows to 10cm [4in] square, measured over Chunky Garter Stitch Pattern using 5mm [US8] ndls.

To knit a tension square for this project, cast on 25 sts using 5mm [US8] ndls and work in Chunky Garter Stitch Pattern from Row 1 until work measures 7cm [2¾in]. Cast [bind] off. Block your square and then measure it. (See page 33 for more details)

Finished Measurements
Width at widest point 9cm [3½in]
Length from cast on edge to cast off edge 14cm [5½in]

To Fit
Adult female

Abbreviations
See chart on page 127 for specific abbreviations.

Notes

For instructions on rib cast on and rib cast [bind] off see the pages 106–108.

How to make

WRIST WARMER (MAKE 2)

Cast on 32 sts using Libby Summers Fine Aran shade 890 Sunset Sky and 4mm [US6] ndls. Work in k1, p1 rib as foll:

Row 1 (RS): (K1, p1) to end.
Rep this row 11 more times.
*Change to 5mm [US8] ndls and, with RS facing, work in Chunky Garter Stitch Pattern as folls:
Knit 5 rows.
Purl 5 rows.
Rep last 10 rows once more.
Knit 5 rows ending with a RS row (WS facing for next row).
**Change to 4mm [US6] ndls and work 11 rows in k1, p1 rib ending on a RS row.
Cast [bind] off on WS using rib cast off method.

Making Up

Block work (see page 61). Do not press – this will flatten the Chunky Garter Stitch.
The cast on edge is the wrist end of your wrist warmer. Place each piece on a table and fold work in half lengthways, so left side and right side of

work meet with the WS on the inside. Place a marker (use a pin or a piece of contrasting yarn) just underneath the top rib section. Place another marker 4.5cm [1¾in] down from first marker. These markers mark the position of the thumb hole. Sew up the side seam (ie. where left and right sides meet) using mattress stitch (see page 62), leaving out the section marked for the thumb. It's best to fasten yarn off when you come to the first marker, and then rejoin another piece of yarn at the second marker. Alternatively, sew the seam up using back stitch, but remember to turn the work around so the RSs are tog while sewing up.

Two colour version

Cast on 32 sts using Yarn B and 4mm [US6] ndls using rib method (see notes).

Work in k1, p1 rib as foll:
Row 1 (RS): (K1, p1) rep to end.
Change to yarn A (see page 50 for details of changing colour).
Next row (WS): Purl.
Cont in Yarn A, work 10 more rows in k1, p1 rib, ending with a WS row.

Cont as for single colour wrist warmers from * to **.
Change to 4mm [US6] ndls and work 10 rows in k1, p1 rib ending with a RS row.
Change to Yarn B.
Next row (WS): Purl.
Work one row in k1, p1 rib.
Cast [bind] off on WS using rib cast off method.

TEXTURE 1: ADDING TEXTURE AND PATTERN TO YOUR WORK

Combining Knit and Purl

There are so many different ways of combining knit and purl to create texture that a whole book could be filled with all the different stitch patterns that could be created from just these two stitches. Some knitters are content with these skills and never progress beyond this stage or spend years knitting at this level before attempting cable, bobbles and so on. This is not because these other techniques are impossibly hard but simply because there is so much to explore with these basics. Below are some examples of common stitch patterns, with instructions.

Knit and Purl Garter Stitch
(any number of sts; 10 Rows)
Knit 5 rows.
Purl 5 rows.
Rep last 10 rows.

Stocking Stitch and Garter Stitch Panels
(multiple of 6 sts plus 3 sts; 2 Rows)
Row 1 (RS): (K3, p3) rep to last 3 sts, k3.
Row 2: P.

Double Moss [Seed] Panels (Multiple of 6 sts; 4 Rows)
Row 1 (RS): (P1, k1) three times.
Row 2: As row 1.
Row 3: (P2, k1) twice.
Row 4: (P1, k2) twice.

Basket Stitch (multiple of 8 sts; 8 Rows)
Row 1 (RS): (K4, p4) rep to end.
Rep row 1 three times more.
Row 5 (RS): (P4, k4) rep to end.
Rep row 5 three times more.

Broken Rib (even number of stitches; 2 Rows)
Row 1 (RS): (K1, p1) rep to end.
Row 2: Purl.

Moss [Seed] Stitch (even number of stitches; 2 Rows)
Row 1 (RS): (K1, p1) rep to end.
Row 2: (P1, k1) rep to end.

Moss [Seed] Stitch (3 sts; 1 Row)
Row 1(RS): (K1, p1) rep to last st, k1.
Rep row 1.

Broken Garter Stitch (multiple of 4 sts, using minimum of 8 sts; 8 Rows)
Row 1 (RS): K.
Row 2: (K3, p1) rep to end.
Rep last 2 rows once more.
Row 5 (RS): K.
Row 6: K1, (p1, k3) rep to last 3 sts, p1, k2.
Rep last 2 rows once more.

Diamonds on stocking stitch (multiple of 6 sts with minimum of 12 sts; 6 Rows)
Row 1 (RS): P3, k1, (p5, k1) to last 2 sts, p2.
Row 2: K1, p1, k1, p1, (k3, p1, k1, p1) to last 2 sts, k2.
Row 3: P1, k1, p3, (k1, p1, k1, p3) rep to last st, k1.
Row 4: (K5, p1) rep to end.
Row 5: P1, k1, p3, (k1, p1, k1, p3) to last st, k1.
Row 6: K1, p1, k1, p1, (k3, p1, k1, p1) to last 2 sts, k2.

PROJECT 3: ROMEO

Monochrome Cushion Set

These gorgeous two tone cushions look striking in black and white, but other colour combinations would work equally well. Libby Summers Chunky is ideal for home accessories, being soft to the touch and having a lovely sheen.

Materials

ZIGZAG CUSHION

3 x 50g balls Libby Summers Chunky shade 100 Elderflower Cream
3 x 50g balls Libby Summers Chunky shade 500 Yana
Pair 8mm [US11] ndls
One 30cm [12in] x 50cm [20in] cushion pad

ELONGATED BASKET STITCH CUSHION

3 x 50g balls Libby Summers Chunky shade 100 Elderflower Cream
3 x 50g balls Libby Summers Chunky shade 500 Yana
Pair 8mm [US11] ndls
One 30cm [12in] x 50cm [20in] cushion pad

TENSION

12 sts and 15 rows to 10cm [4in] square, measured over stocking [stockinette] stitch using 8mm [US11] ndls.

To knit a tension square for this project, cast on 16 sts using 8mm [US11] ndls and work in stocking [stockinette] stitch until work measures 12cm [4¾in]. Cast [bind] off. Block your square and then measure it. (See page 33 for more details)

Finished Measurements
30cm [12in] x 50cm [20in]

To fit
30cm [12in] x 50cm [20in] cushion pad

Abbreviations
See chart on page 127 for specific abbreviations.

Note for beginners

As an alternative to reading from the chart, the pattern is written out opposite. If you are new to charts, refer to page 98–9 for instructions on chart reading. You might also find it helpful to follow the written instructions opposite in conjunction with the chart to help gain fluency in reading them. Another way to learn would be to knit one cushion using the written instructions and then a second, following the chart.

How to make
ZIGZAG CUSHION

Front

Cast on 36 sts using Libby Summers Chunky shade 100 Elderflower Cream and 8mm [US11] ndls.
Work from Chart, rep 16 row patt until work meas 50cm [19¾in], ending with a WS row.
Cast [bind] off.

Row 1 (RS): (P1, k1, p1, k4) rep to last st, p1.
Row 2: K1, (p4, k1, p1, k1) rep to end.
Row 3: K1, (p1, k1, p1, k4) rep to end.
Row 4: (P4, k1, p1, k1) rep to last st, p1.
Row 5: K2, (p1, k1, p1, k4) rep to last 6 sts, p1, k1, p1, k3.
Row 6: P3, (k1, p1, k1, p4) rep last 5 sts, k1, p1, k1, p2.
Row 7: K3, (p1, k1, p1, k4) rep to last 5 sts, p1, k1, p1, k2.
Row 8: P2, (k1, p1, k1, p4) rep to last 6 sts, k1, p1, k1, p3.
Row 9: (K4, p1, k1, p1) rep to last st, k1.
Row 10: P1, (k1, p1, k1, p4) rep to end.
Row 11: As Row 7.
Row 12: As Row 8.

Row 13: As Row 5.
Row 14: As Row 6.
Row 15: As Row 3.
Row 16: As Row 4.
Rep 16 row patt until work meas 50cm [19¾in]. Cast off.

ZIGZAG CUSHION
Back (make 2 pieces the same)
Cast on 36 sts using Libby Summers Chunky shade 500 Yana and 8mm [US11] ndls.
Work in rib patt as folls:
Row 1 (RS): (K3, p3) rep to end. Rep this row 9 times more (10 rows altogether). The first row is the RS.
Work in st st, starting with a knit row, until st st section meas 25cm [10in].
Cast [bind] off.

Making Up
Block work (see page 61). Do not press – this will flatten the raised pattern.

Place the front piece on a table with WS of work facing downwards, and RS facing you with the cast on end nearest to you, and place the two back pieces on top with WS facing you, so that cast off edge of one is nearest to you and cast off edge of the other is furthest away from you, and rib sections overlap in the centre. Check the rib sections are exactly aligned and pin these together. Then pin the back and front pieces together all the way around the outside edges of the cushion. Sew around the edge using back stitch (see page 63).
Turn the cushion the right way round, and place the cushion pad inside.

39

Elongated Basket Stitch Cushion

Front

Work as for Zigzag Cushion, using Elongated Basket Stitch Design Chart instead of Zigzag Chart for the front, and using 500 Yana instead of 100 Elderflower Cream.

If you prefer to read written instructions rather than reading from a chart, the pattern is written out for you. Rep the 4 row pattern until work meas 50cm [19¾in].

Row 1 (RS): (P6, k6) rep to end.
Row 2: As Row 1.
Row 3: (K6, p6) rep to end.
Row 4: As Row 3.

Back

Work the Back the same as Zigzag Cushion Back, but using 100 Elderflower Cream.

Making Up

Make up as for Zigzag Cushion.

Knitting instructions

Work from right to left on RS rows and left to right on WS rows.

Monochrome cushion set zigzag design

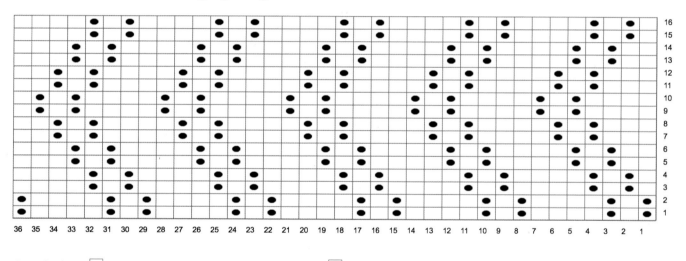

Symbols   ☐ Knit on RS rows, Purl on WS rows   ● Purl on RS rows, Knit on WS rows

Monochrome cushion elongated basket stitch design

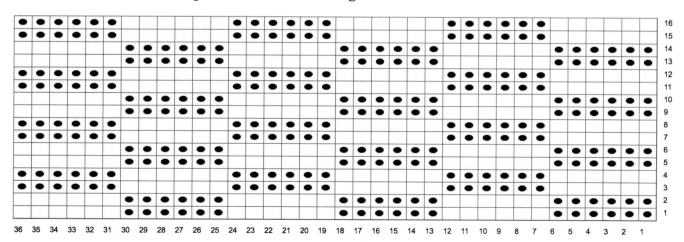

SHAPE 1: DECREASING AND INCREASING

Decreasing

Removing one or more stitches from either end or both ends of a row changes the shape of your knitting at the edges. Taking stitches away at regular intervals along a row gives the fabric a three dimensional shape. Decreasing can be done right at the edge of the fabric or one or two stitches in from the edge. The latter draws attention to the stitches worked and means that sewing up is easier because the edge stitch will be the same all the way up the work. This decrease can also be decorative, adding attractive detail to the design. However, where both shape and a continuous even fabric is required, decreasing should be done right at the edge of the fabric.

Examples of two common right side decreases are given below. Decrease stitches lean either to the left or the right so if you are decreasing at each end of a row you should use one of each for symmetry. Decreasing can also be done on the wrong side, but is less common.

Slip one, knit one, pass slipped stitch over (skpo)

Fig 1 below demonstrates decreasing at the beginning of a row two stitches in from the edge using 'skpo' technique, which creates a left leaning decrease.

STEP 1
Knit 2 sts and slip the third stitch to the RH needle

STEP 2
Knit the next stitch

STEP 3
Reach over the st just knitted to grab hold of the slipped st with your LH needle

STEP 4
Pass this st over the top of the st closest to the tip of your needle. 4 sts become 3 sts.

FIG 1
The appearance of a left leaning decrease, created by skpo

41

Knit two together (k2tog)

The technique below demonstrates decreasing at the end of a row, two stitches in from the edge using the 'k2tog' technique. This creates a right leaning decrease.

STEP 1
Knit 2 sts, insert RH needle into two sts at once.

STEP 2
Knit these sts as if they were one, leaving one st on RH needle in place of two.

FIG 2
The appearance of a right leaning decrease created by k2tog.

Decreasing at the edge of work

Work as for techniques above, but for first two sts of row, rather than 3rd and 4th, or if at the end of the row, for the last 2 stitches of row, rather than the two previous stitches.

Note

To p2tog, follow the same principle as in k2tog of working 2 sts at the same time, but this time using the purl method described on p. 30.

Increasing

Adding one or more stitches into a row makes the fabric wider. Adding stitches at even intervals along a row on a series of rows gives the fabric a three dimensional shape. As with decreasing, increasing can take place right at the edge of the fabric or one or two stitches in from the edge. Increasing is normally carried out on the right side of fabric becuase it is easier to execute and looks neater. Examples of two common increase techniques are given below.

STEP 1
Insert RH needle into st, yarn round needle and pull through in usual way, but do not drop the stitch.

Knit into front and back of stitch (kfb)

This method adds an extra stitch by working into one stitch twice.

STEP 2
Take the needle round to the back of the stitch and knit into the back of it, slipping the original loop off the LH needle.

FIG 3: (Kfb)
The new st appears as a small 'purl' stitch.

Make One (M1)

This method adds a stitch by picking up the loop in the row below and working into it. Work into the back of the loop, knitting on a right side row and purling on a wrong side row, otherwise a hole will appear in the fabric. This technique can only be performed at least one stitch in from the edge. The new stitch appears to grow out of the fabric, meaning that the increase is much more discreet.

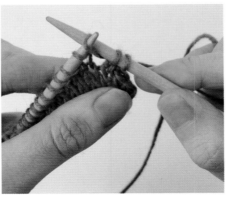

STEP 1
Pick up the loop which naturally lies between the stitch on your RH needle and the stitch on your LH needle and place it on your LH needle.

STEP 2
Knit into the back of the new stitch and drop the loop from the LH needle.

FIG 4: (M1)
The new stitch appears as a small 'V'. This will appear to 'grow' invisibly out of your knitting once you have knitted a few more rows and the stitch is established.

PROJECT 4: BALMORAL

Hot Water Bottle Cover

There's nothing as comforting as a snuggly hot water bottle when it is cold outside. This design combines three different stitch patterns to striking effect, and the flap opening is easy to use. A manageable sized project with only a small amount of simple shaping, this is a great pattern for a beginner who wants to practise their techniques.

Materials

2 x 100g skeins Artesano Aran (photographed in Sunrise CA13, Violet C756 and Deep Purple 3158)
Pair 5mm [US8] ndls
2 litre hot water bottle 18.5cm [7¼in] wide x 32cm [12½in] high

How to make

COVER INSTRUCTIONS

Front

Cast on 29 sts using Artesano Aran and 5mm [US8] ndls.

Work in Moss [Seed] Stitch patt as folls:

Row 1 (RS): (K1, p1) rep to last st, k1.

This row forms patt.

Cont in patt, inc one st at each end of 3rd and foll alt row using kfb technique described on p. 42. Work all new sts in Moss Stitch patt. 33 sts.*

Cont in Moss [Seed] st until work meas 21cm [8¼in], ending with a WS row.

Knit 4 rows garter st.

Work in Seed Rib Patt as folls:

Row 1 (RS): P1, (k3, p1) to end.

Row 2 (WS): Purl.

Rep last 2 rows twice more (six rows of pattern in total).

Dec Row 1 (RS): K2tog, k2, (p1, k3) to last 5 sts, p1, k2, skpo. 31 sts.

Next Row: Purl

Dec Row 2: K2tog, k1, (p1, k3) to last 4 sts, p1, k1, skpo. 29 sts.

Next Row: Purl

Dec Row 3: K2tog, (p1, k3) to last 3 sts, p1, skpo. 27 sts.

Next Row: Purl

Dec Row 4: P2tog, (k3, p1) to last 5 sts, k3, p2tog. 25 sts.

Cont in Seed Rib Patt until work meas 20cm [8in] from beg of Seed Rib Patt ending with a WS row (41.5cm [16¼in] from cast on edge).

Inc Row 1(RS): Kfb, (k3, p1) to last 4 sts, k2, kfb, p1. 27 sts.

Next Row: Purl

Inc Row 2: Kfb, (p1, k3) to last 2 sts, p1, kfb. 29 sts.

Next Row: Purl.

Inc Row 3: Kfb, k1, (p1, k3) to last 3 sts, p1, k1, kfb. 31 sts.

Next Row: Purl

Inc Row 4: Kfb, k2, (p1, k3) to last 4 sts, p1, k2, kfb. 33 sts.

Work 6 rows in Seed Rib Pattern, ending with a WS row.

Knit 4 rows garter st.

Cast off on RS.

Back

Work as for Front to *.

Cont in Moss [Seed] Stitch until work meas 23cm [9in], ending with a WS row.

Knit 4 rows garter st.

Cast [bind] off.

Making Up

With RS facing you, fold Seed Rib section of Front over so that RSs are together and four rows of garter stitch at the beginning match up with four rows of garter stitch at the end. Place Back piece on top of Front piece, making sure that cast off edge of Back piece comes above the four rows of garter stitch on Front piece. Pin in place. Sew pieces together using back stitch (page 63), leaving flap opening. Turn right side out.

TENSION

16 sts and 29 rows to 10cm [4in] square measured over Moss [Seed] Stitch using 5mm [US8] ndls.

To knit a tension square [gauge swatch] for this project cast on 20 sts using 5mm [US8] ndls, work in Moss [Seed] Stitch for 12cm [4¾in]. Cast [bind] off. Block your square and then measure it. (See page 33 for more details)

Finished measurements

20cm [8in] wide, narrowing to 12cm [4¾in] x 33cm [13in] high.

Abbreviations

See chart on page 127 for specific abbreviations.

PROJECT 5: JULIET

Textured Beret

Not all hat shapes suit all people but anyone looks good in a beret and the looseness of the style means they are comfortable to wear as well. This beret looks complicated, but is in fact made up of staggered rib stitches – all just knit and purl. The increases and decreases are carried out at the point at which the rib shifts, which adds to the relief. If you follow the pattern carefully, you will find this simpler than it looks!

Materials

Yarn
2 x 50g Libby Summers Fine Aran (photographed in 101 Coastal Cream and 730 Wild Heather)
Pair 3.75mm [US5] ndls
Pair 5mm [US8] ndls

TENSION

16 sts and 24 rows to 10cm [4in] square, measured over Spiral Rib Pattern using 5mm [US8] ndls. (See page 33 for more details on making a tension square)

Finished Measurements

26cm [10in] diameter (measured when flat)
Brim: approx. 52cm [21in] round the circumference.

Abbreviations

See chart on page 127 for specific abbreviations.

How to make

HAT INSTRUCTIONS

Cast on 94 sts using Libby Summers Fine Aran shade 730 Wild Heather or 101 Coastal Cream, or shade of your choice, and 3.75mm [US5] ndls. Work in rib patt as folls:

Row 1 (RS): (K2, p2) rep to last 2 sts, k2.
Row 2: (P2, k2) rep to last 2 sts, p2.
Rep last two rows twice more (6 rows total).
Change to 5mm [US8] ndls and work in Patt as folls:

Patt 1

Inc Row (RS): K1, (M1, k1, p2, k1) rep to last st, M1, k1. 118 sts
Row 1: (P3, k2) rep to last 3 sts, p3.
Row 2: (K3, p2) rep to last 3 sts, k3.
Rep last 2 rows once more.
Inc Row (WS): (P3, k1, M1, k1) rep to last 3 sts, p3. 141 sts

Patt 2

Row 1: K1, (p3, k3) to last 2 sts, p2.
Row 2: K2, (p3, k3) to last st, p1.
Rep last 2 rows twice more.

Patt 3

Inc row (RS): P2, (k2, M1, k1, p3) rep to last st, k1. 164 sts

Row 1 (WS): P1, (k3, p4) rep to last 2 sts, k2.
Row 2: P2, (k4, p3) rep to last st, k1.
Rep last 2 rows once more.
Inc Row (WS): P1, (k2, M1, k1, p4) rep to last 2 sts, k2. 187 sts

Patt 4

Row 1 (RS): (K4, p4) rep to last 3 sts, k3.
Row 2 (WS): P3, (k4, p4) rep to end.
Rep last 2 rows twice more.

Patt 5

Dec Row (RS): (K2tog, p4, k2) rep to last 3 sts, k2tog, p1. 163 sts
Row 1 (WS): K1, (p3, k4) rep to last st, p1.
Row 2 (RS): K1, (p4, k3) rep to last st, p1.
Rep last 2 rows once more.
Dec Row (WS): K1, (p3, k2tog, k2) rep to last st, p1. 140 sts

Patt 6

Row 1 (RS): P2, (k3, p3) rep to end.
Row 2 (WS): (K3, p3) rep to last 2 sts, k2.
Rep last 2 rows twice more.

Patt 7

Dec Row (RS): (K1, k2tog, p3) rep to last 2 sts, k2. 117 sts
Row 1 (WS): (P2, k3) rep to last 2 sts, p2.
Row 2 (RS): (K2, p3) rep to last 2 sts, k2.
Dec Row (WS): (P2, k1, k2tog) rep to last 2 sts, p2. 94 sts

Patt 8

Dec Row (RS): K1, p2, (k2tog, p2) rep to last 3 sts, k2tog, p1. 71 sts
Dec Row: (P1, k2tog) rep to last 2 sts, p2. 48 sts
Dec Row: (Skpo) rep to end. 24 sts
Dec Row: (P2tog) rep to end. 12 sts

Making Up

Fasten off leaving a thread approx 60cm [24in] long. Thread yarn with a darning ndl, and insert ndl through rem 12 sts. Release from knitting ndl and pull tight to gather (for crown of hat). Sew side seam of hat up using mattress stitch (see page 62). The design of the hat allows for one stitch at either side to be lost to the seam.

PROJECT 6: EARL GREY

Tea Cosy

There's nothing quite as English as a proper afternoon tea made in a teapot. This design is reversible, with the extra pompom concealed on the inside. A manageable sized project with only a small amount of simple shaping, this is another great pattern for a beginner who wants to practise their techniques.

Materials

2 x 50g balls Libby Summers Fine Aran in 101 Coastal Cream (Yarn A)

2 x 50g balls Libby Summers Fine Aran in 730 Wild Heather (Yarn B)

Pair 5mm [US8] ndls

Four 4cm [1½in] buttons, two of each colour.

8 cup Teapot

Pompom makers

How to make

COSY INSTRUCTIONS

Make two in each colour

Cast on 46 sts using Libby Summers Fine Aran and 5mm [US8] ndls.

Work in Broken Moss [Seed] Stitch patt as folls:

Row 1 (RS): (K1, p1) rep to end.
Row 2: (P1, k1) rep to end.
Row 3: As Row 1.
Row 4: Purl
Row 5: As Row 2.
Row 6: As Row 1.
Row 7: As Row 2.
Row 8: Purl.

These 8 rows form patt.

Rep patt twice more (three times altogether). Place marker 2cm [¾in] below last row on both side seams.

Cont in patt, dec one st at each end of next and every alt row until 34 sts, then at each end of every row until 28 sts.

Cont in patt, cast [bind] off 2 sts at beg of next 2 rows. 24 sts

Cast [bind] off 4 sts at beg of next 4 rows. 8 sts
Cast [bind] off rem 8 sts.

BUTTON LOOP (MAKE 2)

Cast on 5 sts using Libby Summers Fine Aran and 5mm [US8] ndls.

Work in Moss [Seed] Stitch patt as folls:

Row 1 (RS): (K1, p1) rep to last st, k1.
Rep row 1 until work meas 12cm [4¾in].
Cast [bind] off.

Making Up

Place one piece of each colour RS together. Sew up sides and top using back stitch (page 63), then turn the right way round and sew up the bottom using mattress stitch (page 62). Do the same with the back pieces. With both pieces of one colour facing you, sew the front to the back at top, starting with and ending with markers. It is best to do this with mattress stitch. Turn the tea cosy the other way round and repeat for the other side. Sew buttons in place at bottom corners of one piece in each colour. Sew button loop in place on other sides, one in each corner.

POMPOM (MAKE 2 – ONE IN EACH COLOUR)

Place two pompom discs together and wrap yarn around them, going through the centre hole on each wrap. When the yarn meets in the middle, stop wrapping and cut yarn. Cut around the edge evenly between the two discs and then separate the discs slightly so that the yarn appears between the two discs in the centre. Wrap a long length of yarn around the centre of the yarn and tie tightly and firmly. Sew pompom onto top of tea cosy using the long length of yarn.

TENSION

16 sts and 29 rows to 10cm [4in] square measured over Broken Moss [Seed] Stitch using 5mm [US8] ndls.
To knit a tension square [gauge swatch] for this project cast on 20 sts using 5mm [US8] ndls, work in Broken Moss [Seed] Stitch for 12cm [4¾in]. Cast [bind] off. Block your square and then measure it. (See page 33 for more details)

Finished measurements

25cm [10in] wide x 21cm [8¼in] high laid flat

Abbreviations

See chart on page 127 for specific abbreviations.

COLOUR 1: JOINING IN YARN, STRIPES, CHEVRON STRIPES

Changing colour

Changing colour is quite straightforward if you follow some basic guidelines. The first principle is the same as joining in a new ball of yarn, which is to always join a new colour in at the beginning of a row (this does not always apply if working intarsia or Fair Isle – see pages 93–8). This means that your stitches are much more secure and the change of yarn will not affect the evenness of the fabric. The second principle is to join the yarn in loosely, without tying a knot. Even experienced knitters often seem to tie knots at the end of the row to join in new yarn. This creates problems when you are sewing up. Knots should never be tied in knitting, even when sewing up. There is always a better way, which is weaving (or sewing) in ends (see page 60).

STEP 1:
Insert RH needle into first st. Take your new yarn in your RH between finger and thumb, with short end to the left, and create an open loop (ie. with no knot).

STEP 2:
Wrap the loop around the RH needle, holding both ends firmly in your RH.

STEP 3:
Knit the st with the new yarn, holding yarn firmly in RH and old yarn end in LH to stop st from enlarging.

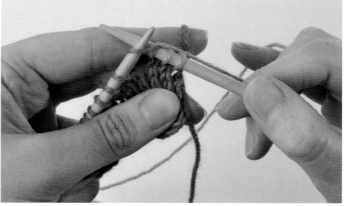

STEP 4:
Continue knitting in new yarn. After a few sts, you can release both short ends of yarn from both hands.

FIG 1:
If knitting stripes of more than one row, continue on the reverse side with the new colour.

FIG 2:
Don't worry about the ends of yarn. You will deal with these when you sew the garment up. Don't be tempted to knot them.

Working in stripes

Stripes can be worked in various combinations. It is usual to have stripes of an even number of rows, so that all your colour changes happen to one side and you can twist the yarn not in use up the side of your knitting, but the number of rows per stripe will be determined by the design. Try practising with even stripes of four rows to start with. Sometimes the end stitch will appear a bit loopy. Deal with this by gently pulling the short end which will make the stitch the right size again.

FIG 3:
This picture shows how to twist the yarns together at the beginning of right side rows. Just lift the yarn not in use over the top of the yarn you are using before knitting the first stitch.

Chevron Stripes

Project 9 uses chevron stripes, which are created by combining colour work with shaping techniques to create a wavy striped pattern. Shaping is spaced evenly across the row, alternating between decreasing and increasing. The position of each decrease or increase is maintained vertically on every other row which creates the up and down shape of the stripes. Colours can be changed either every other row for narrow stripes, every 4 rows or any number of rows, as desired. This is therefore quite a fun technique and pattern to experiment with to create various effects. Project 9 is in stocking [stockinette] stitch, but chevron stripes can also combine stocking stitch and garter stitch to striking effect.

Garter Stitch Chevron Pattern

(multiple of 22 sts + 1st)

Row 1: (for 23 sts) Using Yarn A, k.

Row 2: Using Yarn A k1, skpo, k8, M1, k1, M1, k8, k2tog, k1.

Rep last 2 rows once more.

Rep Rows 1 and 2 twice using Yarn B.

If working with a larger multiple of 22 sts + 1, work patt as folls:

Row 1: Using Yarn A, k.

Row 2: Using Yarn A K1, skpo, K8, M1, K1, M1, (K8, skpo, K1, K2tog, K8, M1, K1, M1) rep to last 11sts, K8, K2tog, K1.

Rep last 2 rows once more.

Rep Rows 1 and 2 twice using Yarn B.

Stocking [Stockinette] Stitch Chevron Pattern
(see Project 9 for pattern instructions)

PROJECT 7: **GWENDOLINE PURSE**

This sturdy little purse is useful for keeping coins, cards or personal items in. There are three different designs given in the pattern so that you can practice your stitches. Look ahead to page 93–9 if knitting the fair isle purse, or knit one of the other two patterns now, and knit the fair isle one later when your knitting skills have progressed. The pattern has no shaping, and is very quick to knit, making it an ideal project for a beginner.

Note

Artesano Aran comes in 100g skeins, so you will be able to knit four one colour purses from one skein, or six two colour purses from two skeins of contrasting colours.

Materials
25g of Artesano Aran for one colour purse.
15g of Yarn A and 15g Yarn B Artesano Aran for two colour purse.
One 10cm [4in] zip.
5mm [US8] ndls.

TENSION

The tension for the main pattern will vary and does not need checking. The tension of your border pattern needs to be checked because this needs to be just slightly bigger than your zip length. You are looking for a stitch count of 19 sts to 10cm [4in]. Remember that when you sew up your purse you will lose 1 st at either end of your row. This is why you cast on more than 19 sts, even though the finished tension of the purse is 10cm [4in] wide.

Finished Measurements

Approx: 10cm [4in] wide by 10cm [4in] tall, varying by 0.5cm [¼in] depending on what pattern you are knitting in.

Abbreviations

See chart on page 127 for specific abbreviations.

How to make

Cast on 22 sts using 5mm [US size 8] ndls and Artesano Aran in your choice of border colour. Work in the border pattern of your choice for 4 rows.

BORDER PATTERN 1

(Garter stitch)
  Every row knit.

BORDER PATTERN 2

(Moss stitch)
  Row 1 (RS): (K1, p1) rep to end.
  Row 2 (WS): (P1, k1) rep to end.

BORDER PATTERN 3

(Seed stitch)
  Row 1 (RS): (K1, p1) rep to end.
  Row 2 (WS): Purl.

Work from your choice of chart, or work 36 rows in stocking [stockinette] stitch for a plain purse.
  Increase one stitch at both ends of first row of chart (24 sts), and decrease one stitch at both ends of last row of chart (22 sts). Tips on how to use the charts are given in the text boxes to the side and at the bottom of the page. Work from right to left on RS rows and left to right on WS rows. Each box represents a stitch, and the chart key explains what the symbols mean. See page 98–99 for further notes on working charts.
  Work 4 rows in your choice of border pattern.
Cast [bind] off.

Making Up

With RS facing you, tuck zip underneath knitting and pin one side of the zip to the cast on edge and the other side of the zip to the cast off edge. Sew in place using thread rather than yarn, using a running stitch. Using yarn and mattress stitch (page 62), sew up side seams of purse.

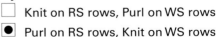

Notes on Charts

Each pattern is an eight stitch pattern repeat. Each purse is 24 stitches wide.
So you need to repeat the pattern three times across the width of your work for each row.
The Stripe and Purl Stitch Pattern is 38 rows, the Fair Isle Pattern and Diagonal Textured
Pattern are 36 rows, not including the border pattern.

Stripe and Purl Stitch Pattern

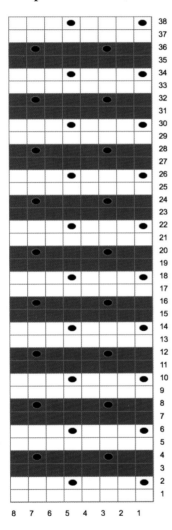

Fair Isle Pattern

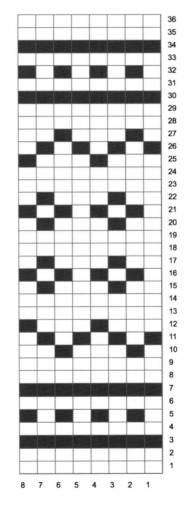

Diagonal Textured Pattern

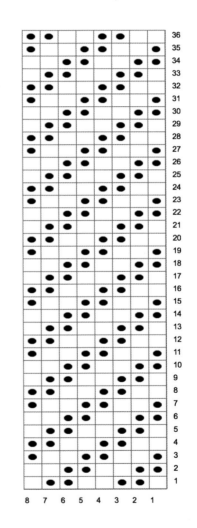

Symbols

 Knit on RS rows, Purl on WS rows
● Purl on RS rows, Knit on WS rows

Symbols

☐ Knit on RS rows, Purl on WS rows
● Purl on RS rows, Knit on WS rows

Symbols

☐ Knit on RS rows, Purl on WS rows
● Purl on RS rows, Knit on WS rows

Yarn Colours

 Yarn A
☐ Yarn B

Yarn Colours

 Yarn A
☐ Yarn B

PROJECT 8: CHARLIE'S ANGEL

Plain and Striped Hat

The original striped version was inspired by the Northumberland coastline with its hazy blues, creams and greys intersected with strips of black rock. I decided to write three sizes to make this a pattern for all the family. A snug fitting beanie style hat, great for keeping out coastal breezes.

Materials

Plain Version
2(2, 2) x 50g balls Libby Summers Chunky shade 434 Misty Day
Pair 6.5mm [US10½] ndls
Pair 8mm [US11] ndls

Striped Version
1(1, 1) x 25g ball Libby Summers Chunky shade 434 Misty Day/860 Clear Skies (Yarn A)
1(1, 1) x 25g ball Libby Summers Chunky shade 500 Yana/100 Elderflower Cream (Yarn B)
1(1, 1) x 25g ball Libby Summers Chunky shade 207 Stamford Stone/007 City Lights (Yarn C)
1(1, 1) x 25g ball Libby Summers Chunky shade 661 Asphalt Grey/008 Alleyway Shadows (Yarn D)
1(1, 1) x 25g ball Libby Summers Chunky shade 860 Clear Skies/009 Evening Horizon (Yarn E)
1(1, 1) x 25g ball Libby Summers Chunky shade 100 Elderflower Cream/661 Asphalt Grey (Yarn F)
Pair 6.5mm [US10½] ndls
Pair 8mm [US11] ndls

TENSION

15 rows and 12 sts to 10cm [4in] square, measured over stocking [stockinette] stitch.

To knit a tension square [gauge swatch] for this project, cast on 16 sts using 8mm [US11] ndls and work in st st until work meas 12cm [4¾in]. Cast [bind] off. Block your square and then measure it. (See page 33 for more details)

Finished Measurements

Circumference 36(46, 58)cm [14 (18, 23)in]
Length from brim to top of crown 18(20, 22)cm [7 (8, 8¾)in]

To Fit

Child (Adult female, Adult Male)

Abbreviations

See chart on page 127 for specific abbreviations.

Note

The number of balls given in brackets in the materials section to the left refer to the larger sizes given in the 'To Fit' section below.

How to make

H**AT**

Striped Version
Cast on 54 (62, 70) sts using Libby Summers Chunky shade Yarn A and 6.5mm [US10½] ndls.
Work in rib as folls:

Row 1 (RS): (K2, p2) rep to last 2 sts, k2.

Row 2: (P2, k2) rep to last 2 sts, p2.

Rep these 2 rows once more, and Row 1 again (5 rows in total).

Next row (WS): Pfb, p26 (30, 34), pfb, p to end. 56 (64, 72) sts
Change to 8mm [US11] ndls and Yarn B.

Work 12 rows in st st, starting with a knit row (RS), following striped pattern as follows:

Row 1 (RS): Yarn B.
Row 2: Yarn C.
Row 3: Yarn D.
Rows 4 & 5: Yarn E.
Row 6: Yarn B.
Row 7: Yarn F.
Row 8: Yarn D.
Rows 9 & 10: Yarn A.
Row 11: Yarn B.
Row 12: Yarn E.

Medium and large sizes only
Row 13: Yarn D.
Rows 14: Yarn C.

Large size only

Row 15: Yarn C.

Row 16: Yarn B

Shape Crown

Row 1 (RS): Using Yarn D (C, A) (K6, k2tog) rep to end. 49 (56, 63) sts.

Row 2: Using Yarn C (B, D) purl.

Row 3: Using Yarn C (A, F) (K5, k2tog) to end. 42 (48, 54) sts.

Row 4: Using Yarn B (D, F) purl.

Row 5: Using Yarn A (F, B) (K4, k2tog) rep to end. 35 (40, 45) sts.

Row 6: Using Yarn D (F, C) purl.

Row 7: Using Yarn F (B, D) (K3, k2tog) rep to end. 28 (32, 36) sts.

Row 8: Using Yarn F (C, E) purl.

Row 9: Using Yarn B (D, E) (K2, k2tog) rep to end. 21 (24, 27) sts.

Row 10: Using Yarn C (E, B) purl.

Row 11: Using Yarn D (E, F) (K1, k2tog) to end. 14 (16, 18) sts.

Row 12: Using Yarn D (E, F) (P2tog) to end. 7 (8, 9) sts.

Break yarn, leaving a long end, and thread with a darning ndl. Gather sts together by inserting ndl through each st in turn, and pull gently to bring them together. Take care when doing this as this yarn breaks easily when pulled too hard.

Making Up

Because of its three dimensional shape, it is difficult to block a hat. Instead lightly press the edges of the hat prior to sewing up, under a damp tea towel, taking care not to press the rib sections. Sew in the ends, following instructions given on page 60. Sew up the side seam of the hat using mattress stitch (page 62).

Plain Version

Work as for Stripey Hat but in Yarn A throughout.

PROJECT 9: MINMAROON

Chevron Striped Blanket

This beautifully soft yarn is 45% silk and 55% merino and has a beautiful sheen and fantastic drape. It is hand wash only, so suitable for a blanket which is mainly used decoratively or as a throw on a sofa. The combination of striking rich colours make this a wonderful centrepiece for any room.

Materials
3 x100g balls Fyberspates Scrumptious DK Worsted Magenta (Yarn A)
3 x 100g balls Fyberspates Scrumptious DK Worsted Water (Yarn B)
3 x 100g balls Fyberspates Scrumptious DK Worsted Chestnut (Yarn C)
3 x 100g balls Fyberspates Scrumptious DK Worsted Moss (Yarn D)
4mm [US6] circular ndl

How to make
BLANKET

Using Yarn A and 4mm [US6] circular ndl, cast on 290 sts.

Border Pattern
   Row 1 (WS): Knit.
   Row 2 (RS): K5, kfb, k4, skpo, k2tog, k4, [(kfb) twice, k4, skpo, k2tog, k4] to last 6 sts, kfb, k5.
   Row 3: Knit.
   Row 4: As Row 2.
These 4 rows form patt.
   Rep Border Patt once more.
Trying to weave/sew the ends in along the edge as you go, cont as folls:

Chevron Pattern
Change to Yarn B, and work **Chevron Patt** as folls:
   Row 1 (WS): Purl.
   Row 2: P4, k1, kfb, k4, skpo, k2tog, k4, [(kfb) twice, k4, skpo, k2tog, k4)] to last 6 sts, kfb, k1, p4.
   Row 3: Purl.
   Row 4: As Row 2.
Rep last 4 rows once more in Yarn B.

Change to Yarn C.
   Work 8 rows in **Chevron Pattern.**
Change to Yarn D.
   Work 8 rows in **Chevron Pattern**
Change to Yarn A.
   Work 8 rows in **Chevron Pattern.**
Rep last 32 rows a further six times (ie. each pattern repeat includes 8 rows of **Chevron Pattern** in each colour, starting with Yarn B and ending with Yarn A).
   Rep **Chevron Pattern**, starting with Yarn B and ending this time with Yarn D (24 rows altogether). You will have eight stripes in each colour, (including the bottom **Border Pattern** in A).
Change to Yarn A.
   Next row: Purl.
   Work 8 rows in **Border Pattern**.
Cast [bind] off.

TENSION/GAUGE
24 sts and 26 rows to
10cm [4in] measured over chevron pattern

Finished Measurements
120cm [47in] wide x 109cm [43in] long.

Abbreviations
See chart on page 127 for specific abbreviations.

FINISHING TECHNIQUES: 1

A huge amount has been written about finishing techniques and, to be honest, a lot of it is over complicated and unless you are doing highly complex and decorative work, you would be best to spend your time perfecting a few key skills. There are just a few staple techniques which you can practise and learn in order to finish your garments expertly and beautifully. You will come to rely on these, and hardly ever need to use any other methods. Practice and procedure are very important, however. Many garments are beautifully knitted and poorly sewn up, which is such a shame after all the work that has gone into making them.

Sewing in Ends

Before you do anything else, sew any loose ends into the back of your fabric. A lot of knitters consider this tiresome but there is some pleasure to be derived from the repetition.

The tutorials below use a striped garment to demonstrate the techniques because the stripes show the stitches more clearly and sewing up a striped garment is more difficult than a plain one.

Thread your darning needle with the end you want to sew in.

STEP 1:
If there are two different threads at the edge of the same row, take one of them to the row below to sew in, rather than sewing both in on the same row.

To sew end in, insert needle through the loop of the first st of the row going upwards, pull yarn through.

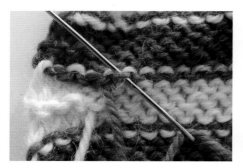

STEP 2:
Go down through the next st loop and up again through the following st loop, pulling yarn through but not too tight. You are only working into either the top or the bottom st loops of a row, not both. In this picture, the bottom loop is being worked.

STEP 3:
Work through three sts in total. Insert needle into 4th st, but before pulling the needle through the loop, insert needle into the external loop first. This secures the end. Trim off the excess yarn without cutting too close.

Four Simple Rules for Sewing in Ends

- Work every end in this way, except for near horizontal edges, never working more than one end into one row.

- Avoid working ends in vertically, horizontally works best except near cuffs and hems, where ends should be taken up the seam vertically to 6 rows away from the edge before sewing in horizontally.

- Never split a stitch. Take care to always insert the needle cleanly.

- Don't pull too tight. Keep the tension of the fabric relaxed.

Blocking, pressing and preparing your garment for sewing up

Depending on the yarn used and the type of project tackled, it is normally recommended that you block your work before sewing up. You might have come across advice that you should also wash your garment or the pieces before blocking but this isn't necessary unless you are working with an unusual yarn, where the finished measurements and look changes on washing. Your ball band should give you information on this. Your ball band will also tell you other care instructions, including whether your yarn is suitable for ironing. Most natural fibers are not or can only take ironing under a damp tea cloth on a low setting. Ironing your garment should be something you take great care over because, unless the garment is pinned to the ironing board, it can easily be stretched in the wrong places. This is one reason why blocking is preferred. It is a gentler process and will not alter your fabric.

Blocking

This book will only cover the two blocking techniques you will probably use the most. Ideally, blocking should be carried out before sewing up. To block your knitted pieces you need large pins, a measuring tape, a blocking board, pin board or foam mats, and a fine plant mist sprayer filled with clean cold water. Dressmaking pins with large bobble ends are fine but you can also buy special blocking pins. If blocking a lace shawl, you might want to use blocking wires too but this is beyond the scope of this book, so you would need to look up how to do it.

Place your knitted pieces on your blocking surface. I use a large cork pin board which is cheap and easy to store. You do need to take care though because the pins will come through the other side, so it is best to place it on the carpet.

Gently ease the knitting out to its final tension – the size you want it to be when you wear it. Do not over-stretch it, otherwise it will be stretched forever. Pin the corners and then the seams in between, lying them as flat as possible on the board and getting the shape as accurate as is possible. When you are happy you have pinned it correctly, take your fine mist sprayer and spray the garment with water. Do not soak it. If you do, it will take longer to dry and will possibly alter the surface appearance of the yarn. Avoid touching the surface of the garment once you have sprayed it. Leave to dry. When dry, gently remove the pins. You are now ready to sew up.

Washing and Drying and the Towel Method of Blocking

Conventional advice is to follow the same blocking process every time you wash your item but blocking a sewn up garment with pins is harder to do. I use the towel method for shaping and drying my garment after washing. Lay a large towel on your draining board and place your washed garment on top of the towel. Shape it carefully. (You can fold sleeves in if there's not enough space for them.) Cover with another towel and press lightly all over to soak up excess moisture. Discard this towel and lay another clean one over the garment. Leave to dry. You may wish to check progress after a couple of hours. If necessary, replace the towels with dry ones and repeat the shaping process. I find this easier than pinning pieces that have been sewn up, but you can follow either method for finished garments. The towel method is only suitable for sewn pieces.

Sewing up Your Garment

There are numerous sewing up stitches you can use in knitting, so I have chosen to include three basic ones which will surfice for most seams.

- **Mattress Stitch**
- **Over Stitch**
- **Back Stitch**

Mattress Stitch

This is my favourite and most used stitch. If executed properly it produces an invisible seam. It is worked on the right side of the fabric, so you can see exactly what it will look like as you work. The seam is quite bulky on the inside, but the neatness on the right side surpasses all other stitches. It is especially good for sewing up side seams, and is suitable for most stitches, whether stocking [stockinette] stitch, rib, garter stitch or textured stitches. When sewing up garter stitch edge to edge, insert ndl through the nearest 'purl' stitch rather than the loops between the stitches. The pins in the photos are just to keep the knitting flat for the photos. Do not pin your work while using mattress stitch.

STEP 1:
Thread your darning needle with the yarn left from your cast on or cast [bind] off edge on right hand piece. Insert needle through loop between the edge stitch and the next stitch in on the first row of your left hand piece. There will be a complete 'V' shape on the right hand side of where your needle is.

STEP 2:
Pull needle through, but do not pull yarn tight. Thread needle through same loop on other side, and then through loop between edge stitch and next stitch on row 2 of left hand side. You should always be working on corresponding rows.

STEP 3:
Once you have done this for a few rows, gently pull the yarn to bring the two edges together. You will see how the edge stitch for each side has disappeared onto the wrong side of work, and now the rib looks continuous between the two pieces. This is why a designer who uses mattress stitch will write the instructions so that the first two and last two stitches will be worked the same on both sides. Continue with mattress stitch all the way up the seam. It is particularly good for matching up stripes. If you sew striped pieces up on the wrong side, you cannot see if you are lining them up properly.

Back Stitch

When executed properly, back stitch gives a neat appearance on the right side. It is a very firm stitch providing a lot of strength for seams which might be put under pressure or be pulled a lot. It is ideal for sewing up seams where you are sewing pieces together which are facing different ways, as in attaching a sleeve, or where strength is required, such as shoulder seams. Before starting back stitch, it is recommended that you pin your pieces together. Back stitch must be worked on the wrong side, so you need your right sides facing each other. Make sure to check that both pieces are correctly lined up before you start.

STEP 1:
Thread your darning needle with yarn left over from casting on or casting [binding] off. Insert needle from back to front, one row/stitch in from the edge.

STEP 2:
Pull through, and then going backwards, insert needle to point you started from on side nearest to you.

STEP 3:
Bring needle through from back to front one row/stitch in from point yarn is currently coming from.

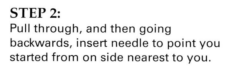

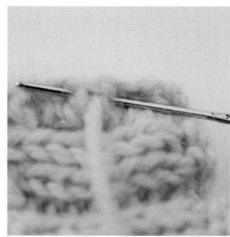

STEP 4:
When you have pulled yarn through you have made your first full stitch, which looks like this.

STEP 5:
Repeat steps above, making sure that when going back, you always insert needle at the point last stitch ends as in the photo above.

STEP 6:
When coming forwards from the back, insert the needle one row/stitch forwards from the last place your yarn went.

Over Stitch

Over stitch is the simplest sewing up stitch and is therefore a useful one for beginners. Unless really carefully executed though, it can look messy on the right side. It should be reserved for rib edges, or seams which won't be on show. As with back stitch, it needs to be worked on the wrong side of fabric.

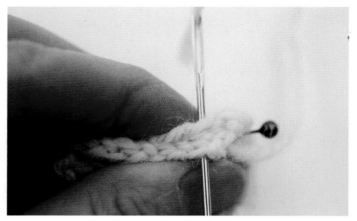

STEP 1:
Thread darning needle with yarn left from cast [bind] off/cast on edge. Insert needle through both pieces of fabric one stitch in from the edge, making sure you insert underneath, not through, the V shaped loops at the edge of work. This means you will be effectively inserting your needle one stitch in from the edge.

STEP 2:
Pull needle through and then start again with the next stitch. There is just this one action with this stitch, which is what makes it simple. But if you split the stitch or insert the needle in the wrong place it will look a mess.

FIG 1.
Compare the picture above of a carefully sewn seam in back stitch, with Fig 2...

FIG 2.
A sloppily sewn seam in over stitch. Choose your stitch wisely!

Picking Up Stitches and Working Neckbands and Armholes

When knitting a garment, you might be instructed to 'pick up and knit' along an edge. This technique allows you to redefine the appearance of the extremes of your knitted fabric, bringing a neater appearance to any shaped edges, as well as often introducing a new stitch for design purposes. Usually this is along the neck or armholes (on a sleeveless top), but can also be used to create cuffs, button bands or even a hem, perhaps if the garment was knitted from side to side rather than vertically. It sounds more daunting than it is and will actually bring you much pleasure as you see your pieces of knitting come together to make a garment.

Step 1:
Insert RH needle under the cast off edge or between the edge stitch and the previous stitch, depending on what you are working on.

Step 2:
This picture shows how to hold your work in your left hand while picking up sts.

Step 3:
Yarn round needle, bring needle through as if knitting in the usual way creating a stitch on the RH needle. Repeat along the edge in the same way building up stitches on the RH needle.

Step 4:
See how the stitches on a shaped edge are brought together in a new clean line of stitches.

Step 5:
This is what the Right Front of Project 17 will look like after you have done the first section.

Step 6:
Once you have picked up and knitted all the required stitches, continue to knit them as normal following the pattern instructions. For Project 17, the first and last 6 stitches are in a different pattern from the rest of the neckband and should be cast [bound] off in pattern.

Sewing in Sleeves

This subject has a page of its own because sewing in sleeves is one of trickiest bits of finishing a garment. There are lots of different styles of sleeves and the method of sewing up really depends on the particular style you are working with. See pages 125–6 for an overview of different sleeve types. The style of sleeve in Project 17 is what is called a 'set in sleeve' which is harder to sew in than a raglan sleeve or a drop sleeve. This is one of the reasons why this project is included in this book. If you can manage this, then you will certainly be able to manage a drop sleeve or a raglan.

Set in Sleeves
(positioning for sewing up)

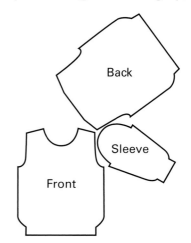

STEP 1:
Sew up the shoulder seam with right sides together using back stitch. Make sure that you have both pieces facing the correct way. Turn the pieces over when holding them together to check.

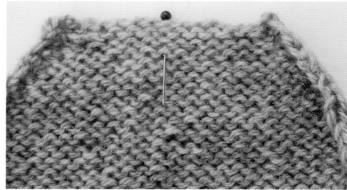

STEP 2:
Find the mid point at the top of the sleeve. This needs to be in line with the shoulder seam when you sew the sleeves in.

STEP 3:
Match the mid point of the sleeve with the shoulder seam and pin the sleeve edge to the front and back edge with RS together. Match the 'cast off 4 sts' sections of the sleeves and armholes, and then pin sections in between evenly.

STEP 4:
Sew the pieces together using back stitch. This is what your work will look like on the RS.

PROJECT 10: ROSINA

Short sleeved Tunic Dress

This pattern is a revision of a popular children's pattern from my Ravelry collection, with refinement to the bodice shaping and the addition of pockets. It works equally well as a dress or a tunic, so if you knit the right age bracket, it will last at least two seasons. The yarn is chosen with this in mind. Cotton yarn is more hard wearing than wool and will also span the seasons. The dress can be worn on its own as a light, comfortable summer dress or with tights over a long-sleeved top during the winter making it a cross-seasonal garment.

TENSION
22 sts and 28 rows to 10cm [4in] square measured over stocking [stockinette] stitch using 4mm [US6] ndls.

Finished measurements
Measured with work laid flat.
Length from shoulder to hem:
46 (50, 55, 63)cm [18 (19¾, 21¾, 24¾)in]
Width at empire waistline:
25 (27, 29, 31)cm [10 (10½, 11½, 12¼)in]

To fit
Age 1-2 (3-4, 5-6, 7-8) yrs

Abbreviations
See chart on page 127 for specific abbreviations.

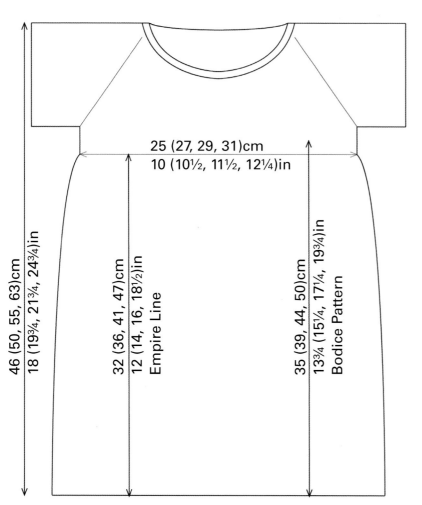

25 (27, 29, 31)cm
10 (10½, 11½, 12¼)in

46 (50, 55, 63)cm
18 (19¾, 21¾, 24¾)in

32 (36, 41, 47)cm
12 (14, 16, 18½)in
Empire Line

35 (39, 44, 50)cm
13¾ (15¼, 17¼, 19¾)in
Bodice Pattern

Materials
2 (3, 3, 4) x 100g balls of Sirdar Knit and Crochet Cotton DK (photographed in 506)
Pair 4mm [US6] ndls
2 stitch holders
Darning ndl

How to make
Front
Cast on 74 (78, 82, 86) sts using 4mm [US6] ndls and Sirdar Cotton DK.
  Beg with a RS row work 6 (6, 8, 8) rows in Garter Stitch. (ie. knit every row)
  Beg with a k row work 12 (14, 16, 18) rows in st st.
  Dec row (RS): K2, skpo, k to last 4 sts, k2tog, k2. 72 (76, 80, 84) sts
  Cont in st st, dec as set on foll 12th (14th, 16th, 18th) row and every foll 12th (14th, 16th, 18th) row to 66 (70, 74, 78) sts.
  Cont straight until work meas 32 (36, 41, 47)cm [12½ (14, 16, 18½)in] ending with a WS row.

Dec row (RS): K22 (24: 26: 28) sts, k3tog, k3, k3tog, k4, k3tog, k3, k3tog, k22 (k24, 26, 28) sts. 58 (62, 66, 70) sts
Next row (WS): Purl.

Bodice
Cont in garter st until work meas 35 (39, 44, 50)cm [13¾ (15¼, 17¼, 19¾)in] from beg ending with a WS row.

Shape Raglan
Work in raglan pattern as foll:
  Row 1 (RS): K2, skpo, k to last 4 sts, k2tog, k2.*
  Row 2: K.
Cont in raglan patt until 40 (44, 46, 50) sts rem ending with a Row 2.

Shape Neck
  Next row: K2, skpo, k11 (13, 14, 15) sts, cast off 10 (10, 10, 12) sts, k10 (12, 13, 14) sts, k2tog, k2.
Turn, working on 14 (16, 17, 18) sts which make up RH side of neck only.
  Next row (WS): K.
  Dec row (RS): K2, skpo, k to last 4 sts, k2tog, k2.
  Rep last 2 rows until 6 (6, 7, 8) sts rem, finishing row at neck edge.
  Next row: Cast off 3 sts, k2 (2, 3, 4).
Leave rem 3 (3, 4, 5) sts on a stitch holder
With WS facing, rejoin yarn to rem sts and complete to match first side, reversing shaping.

Back
Work as for Front to *.
  Cont in garter st, dec as set on every alt row, until 20 (24, 28, 32) sts rem, ending with a RS row.
  Next row: Knit.
  Leave rem 20 (24, 28, 32) sts on a holder.

Left Sleeve
Cast on 48 (50, 54, 58) sts using 4mm [US6] ndls and Sirdar Cotton DK.
  Work 6 (8, 10, 12) rows in garter st.
  Dec row (RS): K2, skpo, k to last 4 sts, k2tog, k2.
  Next row (WS): K.
  Rep last 2 rows until 12 (14, 18, 22) sts rem ending on a WS row.

Shape neck
  Next row (RS): K2, skpo, k3 (4, 6, 8), turn.
  Working on these 6 (7, 9, 11) sts only, and leaving rem 5 (6, 8, 10) sts on a holder, cont as folls:
  Next row (WS): Skpo, k to end. 5 (6, 8, 10) sts
  Next row: K2, skpo, k1 (2, 4, 6). 4 (5, 7, 9) sts
  Next row: Skpo, k2 (3, 3, 5), k0 (k0, k2tog, k2tog). 3 (4, 5, 7) sts.
Leave sts on a holder.

Right Sleeve
Work as for Left Sleeve, until **Shape Neck,** omitting the last WS row, so that you have WS facing for beg of neck shaping.

Shape neck
  Next row (WS): K2, skpo, k3 (4, 6, 8), turn.
  Working on these 6 (7, 9, 11) sts only, and leaving rem 5 (6, 8, 10) sts on a holder, cont as folls:
  Next row (RS): Skpo, k to end. 5 (6, 8, 10) sts
  Next row: K2, skpo, k1 (2, 4, 6). 4 (5, 7, 9) sts
  Next row: Skpo, k2 (3, 3, 5), k0 (k0, k2tog, k2tog). 3 (4, 5, 7) sts.
Leave sts on a holder.

Join Raglan Seams
Join Sleeves to Front and Back on left side and to Front only on right side. I recommend using mattress stitch, with RSs facing and holding work flat to get rows in line.
  With RS facing, knit across 20 (24, 28, 32) sts on holder from Back, k3 (4, 5, 7) sts on holder from Left Sleeve, pick up and k2 (3, 4, 5) sts from middle of Sleeve (the edges of the few rows of shaping), knit across 5 (6, 8, 10) sts on ndl from top of Left Sleeve, knit across 3 (3, 4, 5) sts on holder from left front, pick up and knit 7 (8, 9, 11) sts from left front neck, k10 (10, 10, 12) sts from centre of Front, pick up and knit 7 (8, 9, 11) sts up right front neck, k3 (3, 4, 5) sts on holder from right front, knit across 5 (6, 8, 10) sts left on ndl of Right Sleeve, pick up and knit 2 (3, 4, 5) sts from centre of Right Sleeve, k3 (4, 5, 7) sts left on holder.
  70 (82, 98, 120) sts
  Purl one row.

Knit 3 rows.
Cast [bind] off.

Pockets (make 2)
Cast on 8 (8, 10, 10) sts using 4mm [US6] ndls and Sirdar Cotton.
    Row 1 (RS): K1, M1, k to last st, M1, k1. 10 (10, 12, 12) sts
    Row 2: P1, M1, p to last st, M1, p1. 12 (12, 14, 14) sts
    Beg with a k row work 8 (8, 10, 10) rows in st st.
    Knit 6 rows.
Cast [bind] off on RS.

Making Up
Join rem raglan seam using mattress stitch (page 62).
    Join side seams using mattress stitch, matching up dec rows.
    Position pockets, evenly spaced, on front of dress, approx 6 (6, 8, 8)cm [2¾ (2¾, 3, 3)in] up from hem, or in desired position. Pin in place. Attach the sides and bottom of pockets to dress using over stitch.

TEXTURE 2: BOBBLES, CABLES AND TWISTED STITCHES

More defined and complex textures can be created using specific techniques such as increasing and decreasing, or swapping the position of stitches in the row. This section explores three basic effects which can be created using such techniques.

Bobbles

Bobbles are usually created by working several times into one stitch, turning work to the reverse side and working the same stitches again before flipping back to the right side and passing the extra stitches over the first stitch. This bunches up the fabric in one place, creating a raised stitch or bobble. There are many different methods of creating bobbles, smooth or rounded, elongated or textured. The tutorial below demonstrates a small textured bobble, used in Project 11.

Small textured bobble

STEP 1:
Knit st, but don't slip yarn off LH needle.

STEP 2:
Yarn to front (yf), p st, but don't slip st off LH needle.

STEP 3:
Knit into st again and slip off LH needle. 3 sts on right hand needle in place of original one st.

STEP 4:
Turn work to WS, k and p (k1, p1) into first st, rep for next st. Leave third st unworked, and turn work to RS.

STEP 5:
Slip third stitch left on RH needle to LH needle.

STEP 6:
Pass the other four stitches created from the (k1, p1) in instruction 4 over the top of this stitch, slip st to RH needle.

Cables and Aran Knitting

Cable is a term which usually refers to vertical sections of knitting known as panels in which more than two stitches are twisted together to create relief. Stitches can be twisted to the right or the left, and this variation is used to create interest and definition. Cable techniques can also be used to create all over patterns, with no panels. A separate double pointed needle is needed to create cables. A certain number of stitches are moved onto the cable needle and held at the front or back of work, while a set number of stitches are knitted from the left hand needle, before knitting the stitches from the cable needle to create the twist. Cable panels are often alternated with simpler textured panels or stocking [stockinette] stitch panels.

Patterns may be written or followed from a chart, or sometimes both options are given. The abbreviation for a cable instruction usually begins with a capital C, and the number of stitches to be cabled are given after the 'C' followed by and 'F' or 'B' to indicate whether to hold the stitches at the front or back. Refer to the abbreviations at the beginning of the pattern for specifics on how many of the stitches to put on the cable needle and how many to knit from the left hand needle. Normally this is equal – for example, C4F usually means two stitches are put on cable needle and held to the front and two knitted from the left hand needle – but not always.

As with colour knitting, various traditions have developed over the years of using this technique in particular ways to create distinctive designs. The mostly widely known style of knitting using cables is Aran knitting which is associated with the Aran Islands off the west coast of Ireland.

Cable Pattern 1: C4F. The instructions below for one front cable are given over four stitches, on a background of reverse stocking [stockinette] stitch.

STEP 1:
Slip 2 sts onto cable needle (cn) and hold at front of work.

STEP 2:
K2 from LH ndl.

STEP 3:
K2 sts from cn.

Cable is complete, (p4, C4F) to last 4 sts, p4.

Cable Pattern 2: C4B. The instructions below for one back cable are given over four stitches, on a background of reverse stocking [stockinette] stitch.

STEP 1:
Slip 2 sts onto cn and hold at back of work.

STEP 2:
K2 from LH ndl.

STEP 3:
K2 from cn.

Cable is complete.

Twisted stitches

Twisted stitches are a less pronounced version of cable stitches. The similarity is that the stitches are worked out of order but without a cable needle because only two stitches are involved. Stitches can be twisted to the left (T2B) or the right (T2F). Right leaning stitches are created by twisting stitches at the front and left leaning stitches are created by twisting stitches at the back.

Twisted stitches can be used as an all over pattern or at intervals across the row, and against reverse stocking [stockinette] stitch or stocking [stockinette] stitch or any other pattern, as desired.

Alternate Rib Twist Pattern: (multiple of 8 sts + 2)
  Row 1 (WS): P2, (k2, p2) rep to end.
  Row 2: P2, (T2F, p2, T2B, p2) rep to end.
  Row 3: As row 1.
  Row 4: P2, (T2B, p2, T2F, p2) rep to end.

STEP 1 (T2F):
Reach across next st on LH ndl and insert RH ndl into front of second st and knit, without dropping st from LH ndl.

STEP 2 (T2F):
Knit into first on LH ndl. Drop st and drop second st at same time.

STEP 1 (T2B):
Reach round back of next st on LH ndl and insert RH ndl into back of second st and knit, without dropping st from LH ndl.

STEP 2 (T2B):
Knit into first on LH ndl. Drop st and drop second st at same time.

PROJECT 11: SAPPHIRE

Bobble and Cable Wrist warmers and Hat

The yarn used for this lovely accessories set is machine washable and completely 'itch-free' despite being 100% merino. It is a very strong and elastic yarn, and the wide rib brim on this hat fits snuggly on the head. There are lots of colours to choose from in the range. The pattern is suitable for both men and women, boys and girls, so why not knit a set for the whole family for your Sunday afternoon stroll.

Materials

HAT

1 (1) x 100g skein of Fyberspates
   Vivacious DK (photographed in DK 807
   Deep Aqua)
Pair 3.75mm [US5] ndls
Pair 4mm [US6] ndls
Cable ndl
Darning ndl for sewing up

WRIST WARMERS

1 (1) x 100g skein of Fyberspates
   Vivacious DK (photographed in DK 807
   Deep Aqua)
Pair 3.75mm [US5] ndls
Pair 4mm [US6] ndls
Cable ndl
Darning ndl for sewing up

Note

The cable in this pattern includes a purl stitch and is worked over three stitches. Remember to make sure you bring your yarn forward before purling and take it back before knitting during the cable stitch, otherwise you will end up with extra stitches by accident.

TENSION

21 sts and 32 rows to 10cm [4in] square measured over Diamond Stitch pattern using 4mm [US6] ndls.

Finished measurements

WRIST WARMER

Approx 18 (22)cm [7 (8¾)in] wide and 24 (30)cm [9½ (12)in] high with brim unfolded.

Measurements are taken at widest point (Diamond Stitch). Rib and cable sections will pull in a bit making work appear narrower. When worn, the pattern will stretch to be the same width as the widest section. This is one of the reasons that a cable and/or rib pattern is very suitable for a wrist warmer. Their natural elasticity makes the item a better fit and counteracts any stretch that will occur over time as the fabric relaxes.

HAT

Actual Size Child: 48cm [19in] circumference
Actual Size Adult: 52cm [20½in] circumference

To fit

Age 7-11 (Adult)

Abbreviations

See chart on page 127 for specific abbreviations.

How to make

WRIST WARMER (MAKE 2)

Cast on 40 (50) sts using Fyberspates Vivacious DK and 3.75mm [US5] ndls.
Work in Rib Patt as folls:

Row 1 (RS): (K2, p1, k2, p2, k2, p1) rep to end.
Row 2 (WS): (K1, p2, k2, p2, k1, p2) rep to end.
Rep last 2 rows 7 times more, then Row 1 again (17 rows of rib altogether).
Change to 4mm [US6] ndls and work from Chart from Row 1 to Row 27, starting and ending with a WS row which is read from left to right (see pages 98–9 for more information on working from charts).

Small Size only
Rep Rows 2 (RS row) to 13 (WS row) once more.

Large size only
Rep Rows 2 (RS) – 19 (WS) once more.

Both sizes
Change to 3.75mm [US5] ndls and work 17 rows in Rib Patt, beginning and ending with Row 1 (RS).
Cast [bind] off on WS in Rib Pattern.

Making Up

Block work (see page 61). Do not press – this will flatten the bobbles and cable.

The cast on edge is the finger end of your wrist warmer. Place each piece on a table with RS of work facing downwards with the wrist end nearest to you, and fold work in half lengthways, so that left hand side and right hand side of work meet, and RS is now facing you. Place a marker (use a pin or a piece of contrasting yarn) just underneath the top rib section. Place another marker 4.5cm [1¾in] down from first marker. These two markers mark the position of the thumb hole.

Sew up the side seam (ie. where left and right hand sides meet) using mattress stitch (page 62), leaving out the section marked for the thumb. It is best to fasten yarn off when you come to the first marker, and then rejoin another piece of yarn at the other side of the second marker. Alternatively, sew

the seam up using back stitch, but remember to turn the work so that right sides are together while sewing up.

Hat

Cast on 100 (110) sts using Fyberspates DK and 3.75mm [US5] ndls.

Work 15cm [6in] in Rib Patt as folls, ending with Row 1
Row 1 (RS): (K2, p1, k2, p2, k2, p1) rep to end.
Row 2 (WS): (K1, p2, k2, p2, k1, p2) rep to end.
Change to 4mm [US6] ndls and work from Chart from Row 1 to Row 27, starting and ending with a WS row. The pattern repeat is 10 sts wide, so for the smaller size rep entire chart width once more, and for the larger size, rep entire chart width once more and first 10 sts again.

Large Size only

Rep Rows 2–13 once more, ending with a WS row for shaping.

Both sizes

Shape Crown
Row 1 (RS): [K8, K2tog] to end. 90 (99) sts.
Row 2 and every alt row: Purl.
Row 3: [K7, K2tog] to end. 80 (88) sts.
Row 5: [K6, K2tog] to end. 70 (77) sts.
Row 7: [K5, k2tog] to end. 60 (66) sts.
Row 9: [K4, k2tog] to end. 50 (55) sts.

Row 11: [K3, k2tog] to end. 40 (44) sts.
Row 13: [K2, k2tog] to end. 30 (33) sts.
Row 15: [K1, k2tog] to end. 20 (22) sts.
Next row: K2tog to end. 10 (11) sts.
Next row: K2tog to end (last st) k0 (1). 5 (6) sts.

Break yarn, thread through rem sts using a darning ndl, draw up, secure by sewing a few sts on WS close to top of hat, and fasten off. With RS facing, sew seam up using mattress st.

POM POM
See page 49 for instructions on making a pompom.

SAPPHIRE

Work from right to left on RS rows and left to right on WS rows. Row 1 is a WS row

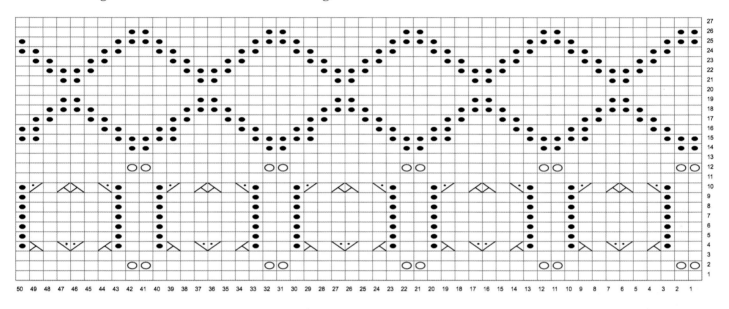

Symbols

☐ Knit on RS rows, Purl on WS rows

○ Bobble (k1, p1, k1) into next st, turn work, (k1, p1) into next 2 sts, turn, leaving 3rd st on LH ndl, once turned, sl leftover st from RH ndl to LH ndl, and pass 4 sts over, sl st onto RH ndl.

● Purl

◹◸ Sl2 to CN, hold in front. P1, k2 from CN

◿◺ Sl1 to CN, hold in back. K2 p1 from CN

SHAPE 2: HOLES, EDGINGS, TUBES AND MORE…

So far we have focused on creating solid blocks of knitting, whether shaped at the edges or straight, and creating interest with texture and colour. To expand your repertoire, you need to learn some more techniques, starting with making a hole. You might have done this already, accidentally – but holes are often integral to your creation. Buttonholes, eyelets, and certain decorative edgings need holes. Lace knitting entirely depends upon repeated patterns of holes. As with shaping techniques, there are a couple of key techniques which we will focus on and again difference between them is in creating a left leaning and right leaning pattern.

Creating a hole – for lace work or a small buttonhole

Yarn forward

On a knit row, if you just want to make a hole and increase the number of stitches at the same time, then simply put the yarn forward where you want the hole and knit the next stitch. On the next row, the yarn forward (yf) will appear as a slanted stitch with no base which you work as a normal stitch. Note, this technique will give you an extra stitch.

Yarn Round Needle

On a purl row, your yarn will already be forward, and just leaving it there will not create a hole as it would on a knit row, so you need to wrap the yarn around the needle to create a hole. Take the yarn over the top of the RH needle and under the bottom to bring the yarn back to the front ready to purl the next stitch. The abbreviation for this is yrn OR yo.

STEP 1:
Knit 3 sts

STEP 2:
Yarn forward

STEP 3:
Knit the next stitch in the usual way.

FIG 1:
Yarn forward, k1. (creating one extra stitch)

Yarn forward, k2tog

This technique creates a hole without increasing the number of stitches in the row while also creating a right leaning edge to the hole. It is commonly used for a buttonhole and can also be worked the other way round (k2tog, yarn forward).

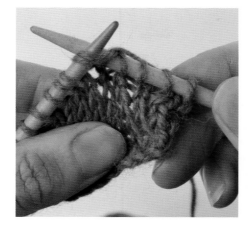

STEP 1:
Yarn forward, then k2tog

FIG 2:
This is what your work will look like

Skpo, yarn forward

This technique is usually used where you want a left leaning stitch before the hole, rather than a right leaning decrease after the hole.

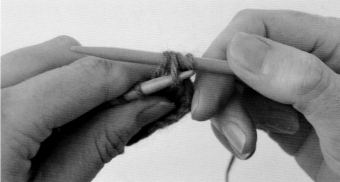

STEP 1:
Slip one stitch, knit one stitch.

STEP 2:
Pass slipped stitch over

STEP 3:
Yarn forward.

STEP 4:
Knit next stitch in usual way.

Picot Edging

Holes can be used to add decorative effect to the edging of your work. Picot edging is the most common, and this tutorial demonstrates a common and simple version of this technique – although there are many other ways and different effects to be created by using the same principles.

Simple picot edging

Row 1: Cast on a multiple of 3 sts + 2 and work 3 rows in st st.

Row 2: Eyelet row: K1, (k2tog, yf, k1) rep to last st, k1.

Row 3: Work 3 rows in st st.

When you come to sew up your work, fold the first few rows to the inside of work, so that the eyelet row creates a wave across the top of work. Over stitch the edge in place on the inside (as shown in Fig 2).

FIG 1:
The top of Project 12 before sewing up, with top folded over. This bag has a picot edging as above and also has an eyelet a few rows below. See opposite page for instructions on creating the eyelet.

FIG 2:
The reverse side of project 12 – sewing the folded top to the main bag using over stitch (see page 64).

Eyelets and Large buttonholes

Sometimes you will want to create a larger hole than a simple yarn forward or yarn round needle produces (page 78). The technique below shows how you can do this over two rows.

STEP 1:
K to the position of hole. Cast [bind] off 2 sts. K to end.

STEP 2:
Purl to cast off point.

STEP 3:
Cast on 2 sts on RH needle, using the thumb method (page 19).

STEP 4:
Purl to end. Eyelet complete.

Short Row Shaping

In the first Shape section (page 41–3) we looked at increasing or decreasing at the edges of your knitting to create a flat shape other than a rectangle. We also looked at increasing or decreasing at intervals in the body of your work to create a three dimensional aspect to your fabric. 'Short row shaping' can be used to create shape by working extra rows on sections of stitches to create curves in your work.

This technique is based around the principle of turning your work before you have finished a row at the point at which you want to create a bend, curve or a slant. To ensure that no holes appear at this point you need to turn your work, slip a stitch and wrap the yarn around the slipped stitch before working across the next row. This is called 'wrapping' a stitch, the abbreviation is 'wrap st', and is demonstrated in steps 3 and 4 below.

STEP 1:
Knit to the point where you want to create shape.

STEP 2:
Turn work, keeping yarn at back.

STEP 3:
Slip the first st from RH needle to LH needle, then bring yarn to front.

STEP 4:
Slip the st back onto RH needle.

STEP 5:
Purl to end of row.

STEP 6:
On next row, knit to one st before the wrapped st in the previous RS row.

STEP 7:
Rep Steps 2–5.

STEP 8:
On next row, knit to one st before the wrapped st in the previous RS row.

STEP 9:
Rep Steps 2–5 again.

FIG 3:
Your work after three rows of short row shaping. The contrast colour was used to demonstrate how the horizontal line of stitches curves upwards with this technique. You can use this in colourwork, as in project 14, or in necklines.

Knitting in the Round

Seams are very useful for defining edges, creating strength and structure, and breaking the process of knitting a garment up into manageable pieces. However, there are certain garments which are best knitted 'in the round' without seams on circular needles. Some designers design almost everything in the round to avoid seams but I believe that seams have an important role to play in creating structure and strength, and when combined with shaping techniques and decorative patterns they can look striking. I reserve knitting in the round for stranded knitting, snoods, cowls and socks. Basically, anything that is mostly or wholly a tube is best knitted in the round.

Circular needles come in various lengths, so you need to choose a length that is appropriate for the size of your project: basically, the smaller the diameter of your finished 'tube' the shorter the needle length.

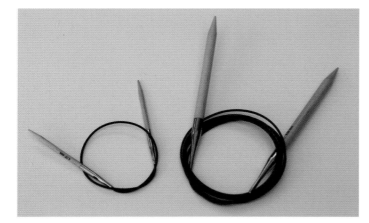

FIG 1:
Circular needles come in all the standard sizes but also in a variety of lengths. Most commonly 25cm [10in], 40cm [16in], 60cm [24in] and 90cm [36in].

FIG 2:
When knitting in the round, the stitches not currently being worked are spread out along the flexible part of the needle, which is often made of plastic.

When you knit in the round, you knit 'rounds' rather than 'rows'. You never turn your work, but just keep going round and round the stitches on your circular needle.

The pitfall with this process is that you can easily lose track of where your round begins and ends. You must place a stitch marker between the first and last stitch of the round. This is where you stopped casting on and started knitting your first round.

Certain stitches are created differently from knitting in rows. For example, for stocking [stockinette] stitch, every round will be a knit row because you are only working the one side of the fabric. If you want to knit garter stitch, you will need to knit one round and purl one round, as if working stocking [stockinette] stitch on straight needles. So it can be confusing to switch between straight needles and circular knitting at first.

There can be a bit of a 'step' between the rows when knitting in the round. This is because the very first cast on row has a beginning and an end, and needed to be joined to make a round. Minimise this by knitting the first and last stitch of the very first row very firmly. You might also try the technique of 'jogging' – beyond the scope of this book, but mentioning it gives you something to look up!

Knitting on Double Pointed Needles

Knitting on double pointed needles gives you the scope to create a much narrower tube than with a circular needle. Ordinarily, four double pointed needles (dpns) are used at once, as in the picture below, with the stitches evenly spread out on three of the needles and the fourth being used to knit the stitches. Make sure you don't knit across more than one needle at a time, otherwise your centre hole will close and you will find it impossible to continue. The principles of the process are exactly the same as they are with circular knitting, working on one side of fabric only and following 'rounds' rather than 'rows'.

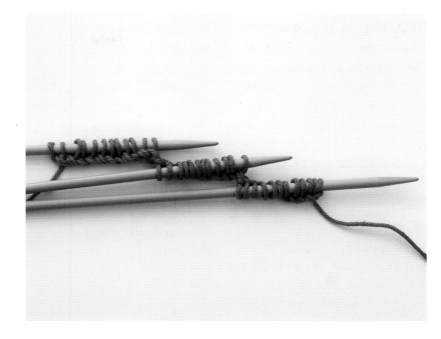

STEP 1:
Cast on the required number of stitches using two needles. Separate out the sts evenly onto three dpns, as above.

Note:

Note in the picture that in the first round, the position of the short end of yarn easily marks where the round begins. As you knit more rounds, this marker will become less easy to follow so it is best to put your own stitch marker on the needle just before the first stitch of each round, slipping it at the beginning of each round as you work. This will help you keep track of how many rounds you have worked.

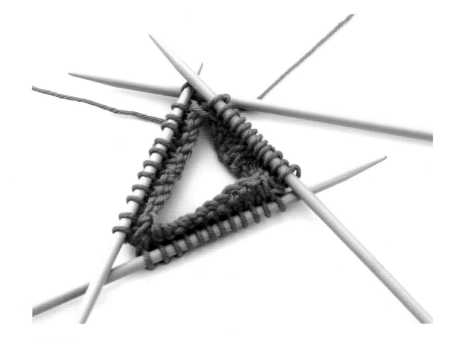

STEP 2:
Join the sts to begin a round by using your fourth needle. Knit the sts from the first needle with this needle starting with the first cast on st. Then slide the sts from the second needle towards the tip nearest to the st you have just knitted, and use the needle which no longer has sts on it to knit the next set of sts from the second needle. Repeat for the third needle. Round complete.

PROJECT 12: ELLA MARIA

Mini Tote Bag

This pattern was designed with my own girls in mind, as a cute little bag for collecting Easter eggs on our annual hunt. However, it is great as a little bag for little people to carry around on any day of the year. This revision of the pattern from my Ravelry collection includes two sizes. You might wish to knit more flowers to cover the bag, or position them differently. The project knits up quickly in this gorgeous cotton yarn which is hard wearing with a beautiful sheen and is available in many colours.

Materials
1 (2) x 50g ball Rowan Cotton Glace (4ply) in Main Colour (MC) (photographed in Shoot 814 and Lipstick 865)
Oddments of Rowan DK Handknit Cotton in two contrasting colours
Pair of 3.75 mm [US5] straight ndls
Pair of 4mm [US6] straight ndls
Pair of 4mm [US6] double pointed ndls (dpns).

TENSION
For main bag, 21 sts and 29 rows to 10cm [4in] square measured over st st (stockinette stitch) using 4mm [US6] ndls.

To knit a tension square for this project, cast on 26 sts using 3.75mm [US5] ndls and work in st st until work measures 12cm. Cast [bind] off. Block your square and then measure it. (See page 33 for more details)

Finished Measurements
The finished bag measures approximately 14cm [5½in] (18cm [7in]) high from the bottom to the picot edge and 13cm [5in] (17cm [6¾]) wide.

Abbreviations
See chart on page 127 for specific abbreviations.

How to make
MAIN BODY (MAKE 2)

Cast on 33 (42) sts using 3.75mm [US5] ndls and Rowan Cotton Glace in MC.

Work 36 (46) rows in st st.
See pages 80–1 for pictures of making the picot edging and eyelets.

Make Eyelet
Next row (RS): K8, cast [bind] off 2 sts, k to last 10 sts, cast [bind] off 2 sts, k to end.
Next row (WS): P8, cast on 2 sts, p to last 8 sts, cast on 2 sts, p to end.
Work 3 rows in st st.

Set picot edge

Next row (WS): P2, (yrn, p2tog, p1) rep to last st, p1.

Work 3 rows in st st, starting with a knit row.

Make Eyelet

Next row (WS): P8, cast [bind] off 2 sts, p to last 10 sts, cast [bind] off 2 sts, p to end.

Next row (RS): K8, cast on 2 sts, k to last 8 sts, cast on 2 sts, k to end.

Work 3 rows in st st.

Cast [bind] off.

Making Up

Make up the main body before knitting the handles. Block work (see page 61 for details).

Fold top over to inside so that row of holes forms a picot edge. Over stitch in place on the WS. Over stitch around the holes for the handles to strengthen and bring the two sides tog. Be careful to do this as neatly as possible, as you don't want these stitches to show. With RS tog, sew bottom of bag up using back stitch. With WS tog, sew side seams of bag up using mattress stitch.

HANDLES (MAKE 2)

The handles are knitted as an i-cord. This is a very useful technique for knitting a thin tube with no seam. See page 112 for photo tutorial.

Using 4mm [US6] dpns and Rowan Cotton Glace in MC, cast on 5 sts.

Work in i-cord for 20cm [8in] (30cm [12in]) as folls:

Knit one row.

*Slide sts to the other end of ndl and without turning the work, knit those 5 sts, pulling the yarn from the end of row to the beg behind the sts.

Rep from * to desired length.

Cast [bind] off.

Feed handle through the large holes in the bag, and over stitch in place on the WS, with ends in line with stitches securing the picot edging.

FLOWERS

The flowers in this pattern are very small, and as sewing petals together would be very fiddly I have created a method which shows you how to knit five petals without casting off, using techniques of passing stitches over and turning work to join petals in the centre. Don't try and make sense of the instructions in advance, just follow them very carefully and you will begin to understand the method as you work the flower.

Using DK Handknit Cotton and 4mm [US6] ndls, cast on 2 sts.

Row 1: (Kfbf) into first st on ndl, making two extra stitches. Drop the second stitch (ie the original slip knot) and pull the short end of yarn to make it disappear altogether. You do this because the original slip knot has a knot at the base which you don't really want to be part of your flower. 3 sts

Row 2: K3tog. 1 st

Row 3: Kfbf. 3 sts

Row 4: K3tog. 1 st

You should now have two petal-like 'blobs' attached to each other in the centre. Without turning the work, insert RH ndl into the centre between the two petals, pick up and knit a stitch, then slip the first stitch over the stitch you have just made so you are left with one stitch on the ndl in the centre of the flower to start the next petal. Turn work so that ndl with stitch on is in your LH. This stitch will form the base of your third petal.

Petal 3

*Row 1: Kfbf. 3 sts

Row 2: K3tog. 1 st

Without turning the work (ie with rem stitch still on your RH ndl), insert RH ndl into centre point between the petal you have just knitted and the petal to the left of it, pick up and knit a stitch, then slip the first stitch over the stitch you have just made, so you are left with one stitch on the ndl in the centre of the flower to start the next petal. Turn work so that ndl with the stitch on is in your LH.* This stitch will form the base of your fourth petal.

Petals 4 & 5

Rep from * to *

Fasten off.

Sew ends in on back of flower and sew onto bag.

PROJECT 13: CHARLOTTE

Cable Cowl

Known as both a cowl or a snood, the tubular scarf is a popular garment due both to comfort and the ease with which is can be made. Knitting in the round allows for a much broader choice of stitch pattern because the behaviour of the edges of the knitting does not have to be taken into account. Easy to throw on, it stays in the same place, unlike a scarf, and can be pulled up over the head if you're really cold! This cowl is designed as a medium size accessory, not snug around the neck but not so wide that it hangs low. The long length of the knitting gives depth, warmth and the folds accentuate the vertical pattern. The Manos yarn is beautiful to work with and easy to wear.

Materials
4 x 50g balls Manos Silk Blend DK (photographed in 2330 Baltic)
4mm [US6] circular ndl 40cm [16in] long

How to make
COWL

Cast on 198 sts using Manos Silk DK and 4mm [US6] circular ndl.

Rib Pattern
Rnd 1: (K3, p3) rep to end.
Work 8 rounds in rib patt as given above.
Knit one round, inc 1 st at beg and middle of round.
200 sts

Now work in Cable and Moss Stitch pattern from chart, rep 40 st patt 5 times in each round. Work from right to left for every round. NB. if you were not knitting in the round, you would be working from right to left on RS rows and left to right on WS rows. Working from a chart is much easier when you are knitting in the round (see pages 98–9 for more information of knitting from charts). Rep 8 row patt until work meas 45cm [17¼in] or desired length if you have extra yarn. Make sure you leave enough yarn to work the last 9 rows.

Knit one round, dec 1 st at beg and middle of round.
198 sts

Work 8 rounds in rib patt as given at beg.
Cast [bind] off.

TENSION
22 sts and 28 rows to 10cm [4in] measured over moss stitch on 4mm [US6] ndls.

Finished Measurements
Approx 38cm [15in] wide when laid flat (80cm [32in] circumference). Approx 45cm [17¼in] long when laid flat.

Abbreviations
See chart on page 127 for specific abbreviations.

CABLE AND MOSS STITCH COWL
As you are knitting in the round, work from right to left on every round.

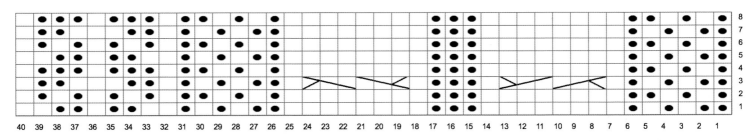

40 39 38 37 36 35 34 33 32 31 30 29 28 27 26 25 24 23 22 21 20 19 18 17 16 15 14 13 12 11 10 9 8 7 6 5 4 3 2 1

Symbols
☐ Knit
● Purl
⟩⟩⟩ Sl3 to CN, hold in back. K3, then k3 from CN
⟩⟩⟩ Sl3 to CN, hold in front. K3, k3 from CN

PROJECT 14: MATUCANA

Striped scarf

This pattern uses short row shaping to create a staggered diagonal stripe, meaning that only one colour is used at any one time. To prevent curling and add warmth, the scarf is backed with a plain scarf of the same size, providing a contrast with the colourful front. This scarf looks great teamed with a plain coat or jumper.

Materials
2 x 50g balls of Libby Summers Fine Aran in 890 Sunset Sky (Yarn A)
6 x 50g balls of Libby Summers Fine Aran in 862 Sea Jewel (Yarn B)
2 x 50g balls of Libby Summers Fine Aran in101 Coastal Cream (Yarn C)
2 x 50g balls of Libby Summers Fine Aran in 660 Sailor's Blue (Yarn D)
2 x 50g balls of Libby Summers Fine Aran in 730 Wild Heather (Yarn E)
2 x 50g balls of Libby Summers Fine Aran in 874 Vintage Green (Yarn F)
Pair 5mm [US8] ndls.

TENSION
18.5 sts and 20 rows to 10cm [4in] square measured over patt on 5mm [US8] ndls.

Finished Measurements
Width: 20cm [8in]
Length: 150cm [59in]
(Approx, depending on pattern repeat).

Abbreviations
See chart on page 127 for specific abbreviations.

How to make

SCARF FRONT

(you must make the front first)

Cast on 39 sts using Libby Summers Fine Aran and Yarn A.

> **Next row (RS):** K3, (p1, k3) to end.
>
> **Next row:** P to end.

Now work in **Patt 1** as folls:

> **Row 1 (RS):** K3, (p1, k3) 8 times, turn work.
>
> **Row 2 and every alt row:** Wrap st, purl to end.
>
> **Row 3:** K3, (p1, k3) 7 times, turn work.
>
> **Row 5:** K3, (p1, k3) 6 times, turn work.
>
> **Row 7:** K3, (p1, k3) 5 times, turn work.
>
> **Row 9:** K3, (p1, k3) 4 times, turn work.
>
> **Row 11:** K3, (p1, k3) 3 times, turn work.
>
> **Row 13:** K3, (p1, k3) twice, turn work.
>
> **Row 15:** K3, (p1, k3), turn work.
>
> **Row 16:** Wrap st, purl to end.

Change to Yarn B and k across all sts.

Now work in **Patt 2** as folls:

> **Row 1 (WS):** P to last 4 sts, turn.
>
> **Row 2 and every alt row:** Wrap st, (k3, p1) to last 3 sts, k3.
>
> **Row 3:** P to last 8 sts, turn.
>
> **Row 5:** P to last 12 sts, turn.
>
> **Row 7:** P to last 16 sts, turn.
>
> **Row 9:** P to last 20 sts, turn.
>
> **Row 11:** P to last 24 sts, turn.
>
> **Row 13:** P to last 28 sts, turn.
>
> **Row 15:** P to last 32 sts, turn.
>
> **Row 16:** Wrap st, (k3, p1) to last 3 sts k3.

Change to Yarn C, p across all sts.

> Work 16 rows of Patt 1.

Change to Yarn D, k across all sts.

> Work 16 rows in Patt 2.

Change to Yarn E, p across all sts.

> Work 16 rows in Patt 1.

Change to Yarn F, k across all sts.

> Work 16 rows in Patt 2.

Rep stripe patt in 6 colours until work meas approx 150cm [59in], finishing with Row 16 of Patt 2 in Yarn F. This may be 10cm [4in] more or less than 150cm [59in], but that doesn't matter, as long as you finish at the end of the 6th colour.

> Cast [bind] off.

SCARF BACK

> Cast on 39 sts using Libby Summers Fine Aran and Yarn B.

Work in st st until work meas the same length as scarf front.

> Cast [bind] off.

Making Up

Block work. Matching cast on and cast off edges, sew Back to Front using mattress stitch (page 62) along side seams and along cast on and cast off edges.

Notes

Wrap st on RS = Having just turned work onto RS, wrap st as folls: ensuring yarn is at back, slip first st from RH ndl to LH ndl, bring yarn to front, slip st back onto RH ndl. Take yarn to back to k next st.

Wrap st on WS = Having just turned work onto WS, wrap st as folls: ensuring yarn is at back, slip first st from RH ndl to LH ndl, bring yarn to front, slip st back onto RH ndl. Yarn is now ready to purl next st.

COLOUR 2: SLIP STITCH COLOUR, STRANDED KNITTING, FAIR ISLE AND INTARSIA

Slip Stitch Two Colour Patterns

In the first colour section (pages 50–2) we looked at knitting with a contrasting colour across a whole row, and briefly at changing colour during a row for easy patterns. This tutorial explores some further techniques for adding more than one colour in one row. Using the slip stitch technique is the easiest way to add a second colour in a row. Only one colour is actually knitted with in any one row, but more than one colour appears in the fabric because the stitch worked in the previous row in a different colour is carried vertically by slipping it rather than working it. Many different stitch patterns that can be created using this technique by varying the number of stitches slipped or knitted or by varying the wrong side row pattern. When slipping stitches, it is important not to pull the yarn too tightly when you knit the next stitch.

Bird's Eye Stitch

(multiple of 2 sts)

Using Yarn A:

    Row 1 (RS): (K1, sl1 pwise) to last st k1.

    Row 2 (WS): Purl.

    Change to Yarn B.

    Row 3: (Sl1 pwise, k1) to end.

    Row 4: Purl.

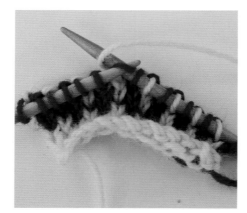 

Row 1 (A is cream)   Row 2 (A is cream)

Mock Houndstooth Stitch

(multiple of 3 sts)

Using Yarn A:

    Row 1 (RS): (Sl1 pwise, k2) to end.

    Row 2 (WS): Purl.

    Change to Yarn B.

    Row 3: (K2, sl1 pwise) to end.

    Row 4: Purl.

Stranded Knitting

Stranded knitting is the technique of creating horizontal bands of geometric patterns in multiple colours. When knitting with two or more colours where the colour changes every few stitches, the yarn can be carried across the work – or 'stranded'. Stranded knitting creates an extra layer in addition to the knitted layer which is made up of the strands or 'floats' of yarn. Traditionally, strands are carried across the back of work but recently a style of colourwork has been adopted in the fashion world which reverses this, so that the floats are visible on the right side. Stranded knitting is almost invariably worked from a chart (see pages 98–9).

Holding the Yarn

Knitters who have adopted the English style of knitting (page 22) will probably find that they will 'throw' the yarn, using their right hand, dropping the yarn not used when they pick up the new colour. Alternatively, they may find a method of holding both colours between their right hand fingers. Continental knitters will hold both colours between their left hand fingers. Knitters who are accomplished in both techniques may find that they can hold one colour in each hand. Experiment to find what works for you, there is no 'right' way. Whatever way you hold the yarn, you should follow the same guidelines.

Guidelines for stranded knitting

EVEN TENSION [GAUGE]

Carry the yarn across the work at the same tension as the knitting. This means keeping a check on your work as you go along, making sure it is neither bunched up on the needles as you carry the yarn across or stretched out too much. Keep the stitches on the needle at the distance they would be when the fabric is laid flat on the table.

YARN DOMINANCE

Yarn dominance means the position of each strand of working yarn in relation to the other. One yarn needs to be chosen as the dominant yarn which is carried across the work at the lower level than the other colour. If you are working with three colours (more unusual in one row), then there will be three levels. Carrying the yarn across at the same level is important for two reasons. Firstly, the layer of floats created on the back will have an even appearance and not be twisted together. Secondly, you will not get your different strands of yarn tangled up and twisted as you work.

FIG 1:
In this photo, the blue yarn will be the dominant yarn for this section of work, and so the contrast yarn (pink) is carried over the top of this yarn.

FIG 2:
When carrying the contrast yarn across the back of work, make sure you keep the tension even.

Tools for Stranded Knitting

There are some tools available to help you with stranded knitting. One of these is a bobbin. If working with small amounts of lots of different colours, it can be helpful to measure out a length of yarn from your ball, wind it round a bobbin and work from this instead of the ball. The bobbin is lighter than the ball, and easier to manoeuvre, and the length of free yarn between the knitting and the bobbin is smaller than the length of free yarn between the knitting and the ball, so tangles or twists are less likely to occur, or can be easily sorted. If you are really keen, and are a continental knitter, you can get a knitting thimble, or Strickfingerhut, which is a guide for holding yarn on your left finger.

Tips for Stranded Knitting

- Knitting in the round is easier than knitting flat, as you do not have to work the purl side (see page 84).
- Knitting with two colours per row is far easier than knitting with three or more colours. This doesn't mean your project has to be restricted to two colours, as other colours can be used in other rows. Scan through the pattern before buying to see if you are going to have to use more than two colours in any one row.
- Choose a wool yarn. Wool fibres tend to cling together, minimising holes or unevenness in your tension.

Cultural Styles of Stranded Knitting

The versatility of stranded knitting has given rise to a wide variety of styles using different types of yarn, processes of working and methods of colour combination. There is a fascinating cultural and historical story behind many of these styles of colour knitting which are usually referred to by their country of origin, such as Scandinavian knitting, Andean Knitting, Fair Isle Knitting and Icelandic Knitting.

Fair Isle knitting has perhaps been the mostly widely used term to refer to colour knitting, and has been adopted to describe all sorts of different types of stranded knitting, to the annoyance of the knitters of Fair Isle. The original Fair Isle style was closely defined, using only two colours in any given row and with patterns limited to two or three consecutive stitches in each colour making stranding quick and easy. These limitations make sense in their cultural context because the technique was developed for practical purposes on a cold and windy Scottish Island. Traditional Fair Isle patterns also use a limited palette of no more than five colours as well as always being knitted in the round. This means the body of the sweater is a tube and 'steeks' are cut to create armholes. Stitches are picked up around the armhole edge and sleeves were knitted in the round to the cuff. Some designers still use these techniques, and have developed them further to create their own unique designs.

TRADITIONAL NORWEGIAN PATTERN

Traditional Fair Isle Pattern

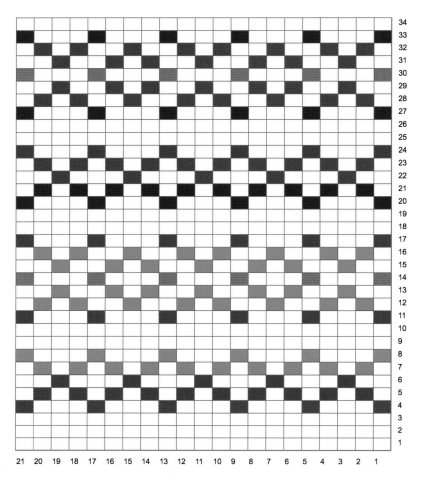

Intarsia

When a pattern calls for separate blocks of colour, stranded knitting is not an appropriate technique. Instead, different sections of colour need to be worked from separate balls of yarn, often wound onto bobbins (see page 94 for more details) for ease. The yarns are overlapped when the colours change to stop holes appearing and keep the evenness of the fabric on the right side. Intarsia techniques are used to create motifs or even for patchwork effects. These might be all over patterns or a single motif on a plain stocking [stockinette] stitch background.

Intarsia knitting is always worked from a chart. The chart opposite is from project 16 and you can clearly see that the contrast colour needs to be knitted in a block, rather than using the stranded yarn technique. The pattern calls for just a couple of stitches for the nose, and four stitches for the eyes. An experienced knitter, or a beginner knitter who is good at sewing, might decide to miss these out and embroider them on afterwards using Swiss embroidery or duplicate stitch. This is an embroidery stitch that recreates the knit stitch precisely on top of previously knitted stitches so the effect is created without having to fiddle around with an extra colour while knitting.

Twisting/overlapping yarns

A word of caution is needed with respect to the process of twisting or overlapping the yarns together on the back. Carry out the minimum twist necessary to prevent holes in your work. If you twist too much, the surface of the knitting will not be even at the colour join. Only twist on rows where you are changing colour at exactly the same point. So in this pattern this will be on rows 5–14 inclusive. On rows where the colour change is staggered, you should not need to twist the yarns together.

Sizing and intarsia charts

Where the same chart is used for different sizes, the chart often extends beyond the intarsia motif, with extra main colour stitches added for larger sizes. Start at the stitch indicated for the size you are working. This might be shown with a darker line down the whole chart or with a bracket around the stitch.

Emily Chart

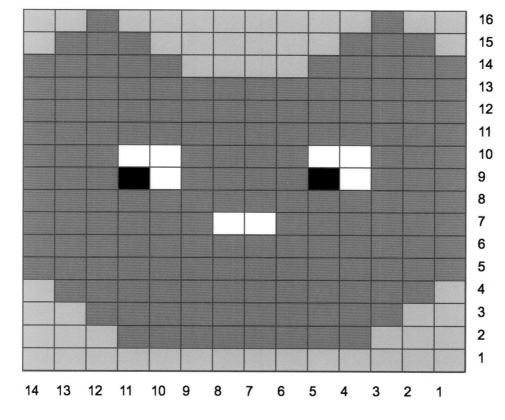

Symbols

☐ Knit on RS (R to L) rows, Purl on WS (L to R) rows

Yarn Colours

▨ Yarn A

▨ Yarn B

☐ Yarn C

■ Yarn D

WORKING FROM CHARTS

Although some knitting charts can look incredibly daunting, the principles of reading a chart are very simple, and often easier than reading written instructions. The number of rows the chart covers are given on the right hand side, and the number of stitches in the chart are given along the bottom. Each horizontal line of squares on the chart represents a row (or part of a row) and each square is a stitch. Unless working in the round, charts are usually worked from right to left on RS rows, and left to right on WS rows, but if a different method of reading is required, special instructions should be given.

Each square will have a colour and/or symbol which will show how it is to be worked such as whether it is knit or purl, cabled or in a particular colour. These are explained in the key. Instructions relating to a cable may be spread over more than one stitch and in this case the key will make that clear. If there is a colour change, this will almost always be indicated by a change in the colour of the square unless the chart is in black and white when shades of grey may be used.

Colour Charts

The chart below (**FIG 1**) is for knitting an intarsia heart in a contrasting dark pink colour on a white background. The key shows the yarn colours, indicating that white (Yarn A) is the main colour and pink (Yarn B) is the contrast colour. The knitting instructions make it clear whether the stitches are worked in different directions on different sides (as in straight knitting) or the same direction (as in knitting in the round). The symbols key indicates that the stitch pattern used is stocking [stockinette] stitch.

This chart would be part of a knitting pattern, for which you would be required to knit further rows before and after the chart and/or further stitches at either side of the chart. There might even be another stitch pattern included in the knitting instructions at the sides or shaping at the edges may be required. Sometimes this is shown on a chart, and sometimes not. It is important to read the instructions carefully to be sure.

FIG 1 Heart

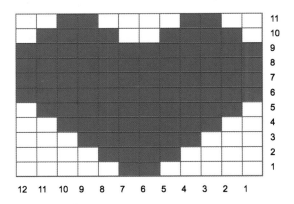

Symbols

☐ Knit on RS rows, Purl on WS rows

Yarn Colours

☐ Yarn A (Main Colour)
■ Yarn B (Contrast Colour)

This chart opposite (**FIG 2**) shows how colour and technique can be both represented on a chart at once. Both shaping and colour changes are required for this chart and the shape of the piece of knitting (a triangle) is shown by where the colour stops at either side. The position of the decrease stitches are marked on the chart (one stitch in from the edge) and the techniques used described in the key.

FIG 2 Spring bunting

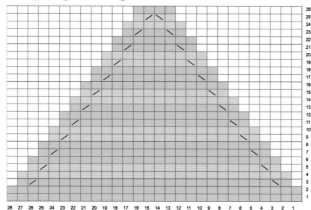

Symbols

☐ Knit on RS rows, Purl on WS rows

◺ Left leaning decrease (skpo)

◿ k2tog

Yarn Colours

☐ Contrast Colour (Pictured as Bleached 263)

▨ Contrast Colour (Pictured as Shade 16)

▨ Main Colour (Pictured as Celery 309)

Knitting instructions

Work from right to left on RS rows and left to right on WS rows

Textured Pattern Charts

Charts which refer to textured patterns can be harder to read and you may find it helps to photocopy the chart and blow it up. The chart below (**FIG 3**) is taken from Project 13 for the Snood. This project is knitted in the round so the chart needs to be followed from right to left on all rounds. This is stated in the instructions. The pattern is mainly a combination of knit and purl stitches, but in the two stocking [stockinette] stitch panels, there is one row with a more complex instruction that spreads across six stitches each time. The key below explains exactly what to do with every one of these six stitches, referring to a cable technique.

Abbreviations and the Key

Abbreviations will be used in the key's instructions and these should be explained in the abbreviations section, usually at the beginning of the pattern instructions. In this instance, the term 'sl 3' means 'slip 3 stitches', 'k3' means 'knit 3 stitches'and cn means cable needle (see page 71–3). An inexperienced knitter may not be able to see how the cable instructions radically alter the appearance of the finished project, but if they were missed out, the result would be simple stocking [stockinette] stitch panels. Including the cables results in lovely curvy wavy lines, which add depth to the knitting and also affect the finished tension by pulling the knitting in. See page 88 for a photograph of the lovely knitting that results from working this chart.

FIG 3 Charlotte

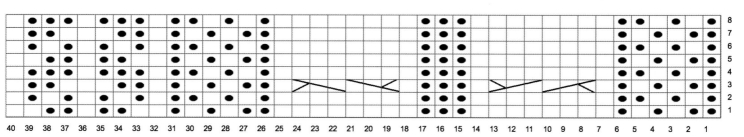

Symbols

☐ Knit

⬤ Purl

◩◩◩ Sl3 to CN, hold in back. K3, then k3 from CN

◩◩◩ Sl3 to CN, hold in front. K3, k3 from CN

PROJECT 15: **SWEET PEA**

Bag

This project is ideal for practising Fair Isle techniques. The pattern is designed for ease of knitting with a maximum of three stitches to carry yarn across, and only two colours on any given row. It also has straight sides, you can really concentrate on the stranded knitting while you work. The effect is striking, and the added lining gives depth to the design as well as making the bag sturdy and practical. Great for making a statement on evenings out. It also happens to be the perfect size for keeping your knitting in so could be used as a project bag. See page 93 for instructions on stranded knitting.

Materials

Yarn

3 x 25g balls Libby Summers Fine Aran 660 Sailor's Blue (Yarn A)
1 x 25g ball Libby Summers Fine Aran 862 Sea Jewel (Yarn B)
1 x 25g ball Libby Summers Fine Aran 890 Sunset Sky (Yarn C)
1 x 25g ball Libby Summers Fine Aran 101 Coastal Cream (Yarn D)
1 x 25g ball Libby Summers Fine Aran 874 Vintage Green (Yarn E)
1 x 25g ball Libby Summers Fine Aran 730 Wild Heather (Yarn F)
Pair 4.5mm [US7] ndls.

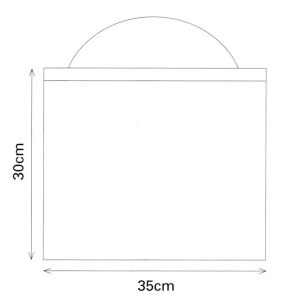

30cm

35cm

TENSION

24 sts and 20 rows to 10cm [4in] square, measured over Fair Isle patt using 4.5mm [US7] ndls.

To knit a tension square for this project, cast on 17 sts using 4.5mm [US7] ndls and work in Fair Isle pattern from chart until work measures 12cm [4¾in]. Cast [bind] off. Block your square and then measure it. (See page 33 for more details.)

Finished Measurements

35cm [13¾in] wide
32cm [12½in] high

Abbreviations

See chart page 127 for specific abbreviations.

How to make

Outer Bag

Cast on 84 sts using Libby Summers Fine Aran shade 660 Sailor's Blue (Yarn C) and 4.5mm [US7] ndls.

Work from chart, rep 12 st patt seven times across the row, and working from right to left on RS rows and left to right on WS rows.

Complete 40 row patt twice. Cast [bind] off in shade 874 Vintage Green (Yarn E).

Lining

Cast on 66 sts using Libby Summers Fine Aran shade 660 Sailor's Blue (Yarn A) and 4.5mm [US7] ndls.

Work in moss [seed] stitch as folls:

Row 1 (RS): (K1, p1) rep to end.
Row 2: (P1, k1) rep to end.
Work 10 rows in moss [seed] stitch altogether.

Begin with RS row, work in st st for 34cm [13½in].

Work 10 rows in moss [seed] stitch as given at beg.

Cast [bind] off.

Handles (make 2)

Cast on 14 sts using Libby Summers Fine Aran shade 660 Sailor's Blue (Yarn C) and 4.5mm [US7] ndls.

Work in rib patt as folls:

Row 1: (K1, p1) rep to end.
Rep Row 1 until work meas 32cm [12½in].

Cast off [bind off].

Making Up

Follow the instructions on page 61 for blocking your work.

With WS facing, fold handle in half width ways, and sew edge to edge using over stitch. Leave ends open. Turn the right way round (a knitting ndl might be useful here). Flatten handle so that seam is central on one side. Back stitch along each edge to strengthen handle, concealing sts in the purl column of the rib patt.

Outer Bag

Fold your work in half so that the cast on and cast [bind] off edges meet and the RS are together (wrong side will be facing you). Sew the side seams together using back stitch (see page 63) leaving cast on and cast off edges open. Turn right way round.

Lining

Make up exactly as for Outer Bag.

Putting the Lining and Outer Bag together.

Turn the lining bag the wrong way out, so that wrong sides are facing you.

Slip the lining inside the outer bag. The moss [seed] stitch section should be visible above the edges of the outer bag. Fold the moss [seed] stitch section to the outside so that the cast on and cast off edges meet the cast on and cast off edges of the outer bag. Sew the two edges together using mattress stitch. Attach the handles inside the bag, with each end positioned approx 6cm [2½in] in from each side seam and 4cm [1½in] down from top of bag. Over stitch in place, taking stitches up sides of handle to point where they are visible at top of bag.

Fair Isle Bag

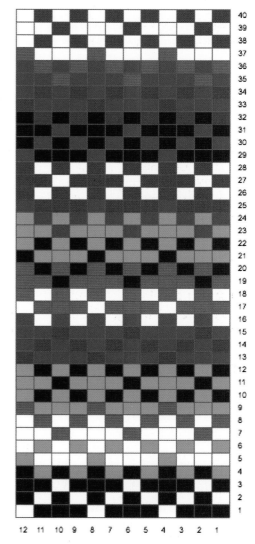

Symbols

☐ Knit on RS rows, Purl on WS rows

Yarn Colours

■ Yarn A (Sailor's Blue 660)
■ Yarn B (Sea Jewel 862)
■ Yarn C (Sunset Sky 890)
☐ Yarn D (Coastal Cream 101)
■ Yarn E (Vintage Green 874)
■ Yarn F (Wild Heather 730)

PROJECT 16: EMILY

Boxy Cardigan with cheeky cats

This cardigan is sure to bring a cheeky smile to your face. A boxy relaxed shape and soft easy to wear yarn make this an ideal choice for spring. Working a repeated chart across a row is good practice in intarsia techniques. If it looks a bit daunting, practise knitting the cats by working the first 22 rows of the sleeves first.

Materials

2 (3, 3, 4, 4, 5) 50g balls Sublime Extra Fine Merino DK Yarn A (photographed in 343 Avalanche

1 (1, 1, 1, 1, 2) 50g balls Sublime Extra Fine Merino DK Yarn B (photographed in 373 Pumpkin

1 (1, 1, 1, 1, 1) 50g balls Sublime Extra Fine Merino DK Yarn C (photographed in 003 Alabaster

1 (1, 1, 1, 1, 1) 50g balls Sublime Extra Fine Merino DK Yarn D (photographed in 013 Jet Black

Pair 4mm [US6] ndls

Set of 3.75mm [US5] double pointed ndls (dpns)

5 small buttons

TENSION

24 sts and 30 rows to 10cm [4in] square measured over stocking [stockinette] stitch using 4mm [US6] ndls.

FINISHED MEASUREMENTS

Measured with work laid flat.
Length from shoulder to hem: 30 (31, 33, 35, 37, 38)cm [11½ (12¼, 13, 13¾, 14½, 15)in]
Width at bottom hem: 31 (34.5, 38, 41, 42, 44)cm [12¼ (13½, 15, 16, 16½, 17¼)in]
Sleeve: 21 (23, 26, 29, 33, 37)cm [8 (9, 10¼, 11½, 13, 14½)in].
The finished chest will be double the width at the bottom hem, so 62 (69, 76, 82, 84, 88)cm [24½ (27, 30¼, 25, 33, 34¾) in].
To fit with 4.5 (6.5, 7.5, 10, 9, 11)cm [1¾ (2½, 3, 4, 3½, 4½)in] positive ease.

To fit

Age: 1-2 (2-3, 3-4, 5-6, 7-8, 9-10) yrs
Chest: 51 (56, 58, 61, 66, 76)cm [20 (22, 23, 24, 28, 30)in]

Abbreviations

See chart on page 127 for specific abbreviations.

Emily Chart

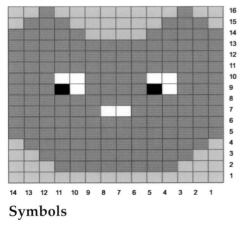

Symbols

☐ Knit on RS (R to L) rows, Purl on WS (L to R) rows

Yarn Colours

☐ Yarn A ☐ Yarn C
☐ Yarn B ■ Yarn D

How to make

Back

Cast on 76 (82, 88, 96, 100, 106) sts using 4mm [US6] ndls and Yarn A.

Beg with a RS row, knit 6 (6, 8, 8, 8, 10) rows.

INTARSIA CATS

Work the intarsia cats as set below.

Size 1

Row 1 (RS): K4A, (work 14 sts of Chart, k4A) 4 times.
Row 2: P4A, (work 14 sts of Chart, p4A) 4 times.

Size 2

Row 1 (RS): K4A, (work 14 sts of Chart, k6A) 3 times, work 14 sts of Chart, k4A.
Row 2: P4A, (work 14 sts of Chart, p6A) 3 times, work 14 sts of Chart, p4A.

Size 3

Row 1 (RS): K4A, (work 14 sts of Chart, k8A) 3 times, work 14 sts of Chart, k4A.
Row 2: P4A, (work 14 sts of Chart, p8A) 3 times, work 14 sts of Chart, p4A.

Size 4

Row 1 (RS): K3A, (work 14 sts of Chart, k5A) 4 times, work 14 sts of Chart, k3A.
Row 2: P3A, (work 14 sts of Chart, p5A) 4 times, work 14 sts of Chart, p3A.

Size 5

Row 1 (RS): K3A, (work 14 sts of Chart, k6A) 4 times, work 14 sts of Chart, k3A.
Row 2: P3A, (work 14 sts of Chart, p6A) 4 times, work 14 sts of Chart, p3A.

Size 6

Row 1 (RS): K4A, (work 14 sts of Chart, k7A) 4 times, work 14 sts of Chart, k4A.
Row 2: P4A, (work 14 sts of Chart, p7A) 4 times, work 14 sts of Chart, p4A.

All Sizes

These 2 rows set position of Chart. Rep rows 1 and 2 until all 16 rows of Chart have been worked.

Cont in Yarn A in st st until work meas 20 (20.5, 22, 23, 23.5, 25)cm [7¾ (8, 8½, 9, 9½, 10)in] ending with a WS row.

Shape Armholes

Cast [bind] off 4 sts at beg of next 2 rows. 68 (74, 80, 88, 92, 98) sts.

Cont in Yarn A in st st until work meas 29 (30, 32, 34, 35, 37)cm [11½ (11¾, 12½, 13¼, 13¾, 14½)in] ending with a WS row.

Shape Shoulder

*Next row (RS): Cast [bind] off 4 (4, 4, 5, 5, 5) sts, k17 (18, 21, 22, 23, 24) sts, turn and work on these 18 (19, 22, 23, 24, 25) sts only.

Next row: Cast [bind] off 3 sts, p to end. 15 (16, 19, 20, 21, 22) sts.

Next row: Cast [bind] off 5 (5, 5, 6, 6, 6) sts, k to end. 10 (11, 14, 14, 15, 16) sts.

Next row: Cast [bind] off 3 sts, p to end. 7 (8, 11, 11, 12, 13) sts.

Cast [bind] off rem 7 (8, 11, 11, 12, 13) sts.

Put central 24 (28, 28, 32, 34, 38) sts on a holder. With RS facing, rejoin yarn to rem 22 (23, 26, 28, 29, 30) sts, k to end.

Complete to match first side from * reversing the knit and purl instructions. (ie k where it says p and vice versa).

Left Front

Cast on 36 (40, 43, 46, 48, 52) sts using 4mm [US6] ndls and Yarn A.

Beg with a RS row knit 6 (6, 8, 8, 8, 10) rows.

INTARSIA CATS

Work the intarsia cats as set below.

Row 1: K2 (3, 4, 6, 7, 8)A, work 14 sts of Chart, k4 (6, 7, 6, 6, 8)A, work 14 sts of Chart, k2 (3, 4, 6, 7, 8)A.

Row 2: P2 (3, 4, 6, 7, 8)A, work 14 sts of Chart, p4 (6, 7, 6, 6, 8)A, work 14 sts of Chart, p2 (3, 4, 6, 7, 8)A.

These 2 rows set position of Chart. Rep rows 1 and

Pattern note

Work the cats from the chart using the intarsia technique described on pages 96–7, overlapping the yarns at the point of the colour change to prevent a gap. When following chart, work from right to left on RS rows and left to right on WS rows.

2 until all 16 rows of Chart have been worked.

Cont in Yarn A in st st until work meas 20 (20.5, 22, 23, 23.5, 25)cm [7¾ (8, 8½, 9, 9½, 10)in] ending with RS facing for next row.

Shape Armhole

Cast [bind] off 4 sts at beg of next row. 32 (36, 39, 42, 44, 48) sts.

Cont in Yarn A in st st until work meas 25 (26, 27, 28, 29, 30)cm [10 (10¼, 10½, 11, 11½, 12)in] ending with a RS row.

Shape Front Neck

Next row (WS): Cast [bind] off 4 (6, 6, 6, 6, 7) sts, p to end. 28 (30, 33, 36, 38, 41) sts.

Next row (RS): K to last 2 sts, k2tog. 27 (29, 32, 35, 37, 40) sts.

Next row: Cast [bind] off 3 (4, 4, 4, 5, 5) sts, p to end. 24 (25, 28, 31, 32, 35) sts.

Next row: K to last 2 sts, k2tog. 23 (24, 27, 30, 31, 34) sts.

Next row: Cast [bind] off 3 sts, p to end. 20 (21, 24, 27, 28, 31) sts.

Next row: K to last 2 sts, k2tog. 19 (20, 23, 26, 27, 30) sts.

Next row: Cast [bind] off 2 sts, p to end. 17 (18, 21, 24, 25, 28) sts.

Next row: K to last 2 sts, k2tog. 16 (17, 20, 23, 24, 27) sts.

Next row: Purl.

Sizes 4-6 only
Rep last 2 rows once more. 22 (23, 26) sts.

All sizes
Meas work against Back, and if shorter than Back to beg shoulder shaping, cont in Yarn A in st st until work meas same as Back to beg shoulder shaping, ending with a WS row.
Next row (RS): Cast [bind] off 4 (4, 4, 5, 5, 5) sts, k to end. 12 (13, 16, 17, 18, 21) sts.
Next row: Purl.
Next row: Cast [bind] off 5 (5, 5, 6, 6, 6) sts, k to end. 7 (8, 11, 11, 12, 15) sts.
Next row: Purl.
Cast [bind] off rem 7 (8, 11, 11, 12, 15) sts.

Right Front
Work as for Left Front reversing shaping. Set position of cats as for left front.
The first point you need to reverse the shaping is at the armholes. End with WS facing for first row of shaping (one row less than for Right Front), and thus work every row after that on the opposite side of work.

Sleeves (make 2)
Cast on 33 (35, 37, 39, 41, 43) sts using 4mm ndls and Yarn A.
Beg with a RS row knit 6 (6, 8, 8, 8, 10) rows.

INTARSIA CATS
Work the intarsia cats as set below.
Row 1: K1(2, 2, 3, 4, 4)A, work 14 sts of Chart, k3 (3, 5, 5, 5, 7)A, work 14 sts of Chart, k1 (2, 2, 3, 4, 4)A.
Row 2: P1(2, 2, 3, 4, 4)A, work 14 sts of Chart, p3 (3, 5, 5, 5, 7)A, work 14 sts of Chart, p1 (2, 2, 3, 4, 4)A.
These 2 rows set the position of Chart. Rep rows 1 and 2 until all 16 rows of Chart have been worked. AT THE SAME TIME inc 1 st at each end of Row 3 and every foll 4th row until 61 (63, 67, 71, 73, 77) sts. Work extra sts in Yarn A, and row 17 onwards in st st in Yarn A.

Cont in st st without shaping until work meas 21 (23, 26, 29, 33, 37)cm [8 (9, 10¼, 11½, 13, 14½)in]. Cast [bind] off.

Making up
Join shoulder seams using back stitch. Mark central point of cast off edge of Sleeve and with RS tog pin sleeves to front and back pieces, matching marker with shoulder seams, and sew tog with back stitch. With RS facing, join sleeve seams and side seams using mattress stitch. Embroider whiskers and a mouth on the cats using a darning ndl and Yarn D.

Button band
With 3.75mm dpns and Yarn A cast on 5 sts. Work i-cord, joining i-cord to cardigan as you go along using the technique described on page 112. Start at top of Left Front and work down to cast on edge before casting [binding] off.

Buttonhole band
Mark the position of buttonholes on the main body of garment before starting using pins. Space them evenly up right front with first buttonhole positioned 3 rows up from bottom edge and last buttonhole positioned 2 rows before casting [binding] off. With 3.75mm dpns and Yarn A cast on 5 sts. Work i-cord, joining i-cord to cardigan as you go along using the technique described on page 112 and working the buttonholes as instructed in the tutorial on page 113. Start on RS at bottom of Right Front and work up to beg of neck shaping before casting off.

Neckband
With 3.75mm dpns and Yarn A cast on 5 sts. Work i-cord, joining i-cord to cardigan as you go along using the technique described on page 112–3. With RS facing start at top of buttonhole band, working at a right angle to cast [bind] off edge, and joining i-cord to cast [bind] off edge of buttonhole band. Work all the way across right neck shaping, across back of neck and across top of button band before casting [binding] off.

FINISHING TECHNIQUES: 2

The techniques already taught are perfectly good for almost all projects. However, if you would like to refine the finish of your knitting, there are further techniques to learn. This section begins with techniques which create a different appearance on the cast on and cast [bind] off selvedge and give a better finish to rib sections with the right amount of elasticity. This is followed by some useful i-cord edging techniques.

Rib Cast on

Make your first stitch in the usual way, with a slip knot.

*Insert needle kwise into st, wrap yarn around needle as if going to knit it, pull the loop through and put loop on LH needle to form a st. Insert needle pwise into this new st, wrap yarn around as if you were going to purl the st, pull the loop through and put on LH needle. Repeat from * until you have desired number of sts.

Rib Sewn Cast off

Cut the yarn leaving a very long end, at least four times longer than the width of your knitting. With knitted stitches on LH knitting needle, discard other needle, and thread a darning needle with the long length of yarn.

STEP 1 (A):
Insert sewing needle kwise into first st. Pull yarn through, but not too tight.

STEP 1 (B):
Drop st.

STEP 2 (A):
Insert sewing needle pwise into third (k) st.

STEP 2 (B):
Pull yarn through, but not too tight. Do not drop st.

STEP 3 (A):
Insert sewing needle pwise into second (p) st.

STEP 3 (B):
Drop st.

STEP 4 (A):
Taking needle and yarn round back of third st (to the right), then insert sewing needle between third and fourth st to bring it back to the front of work (third and fourth sts now appear as first and second sts on LH needle)

STEP 4 (B):
Insert sewing needle kwise into 4th (p) st. Pull yarn through. Do not drop st.
   Repeat Steps 1–4 until end. Fasten off last stitch.
(Remember that your third st described in Step 2 becomes the first st when you start the sequence again).

Rib Knitted Cast off

There are also knitted cast off methods for rib which will give a nice elastic edge. This one is my favourite. You can use this for any cast off edge – it doesn't have to be ribbed. You could also use it for moss stitch which alternates between knit and purl stitches, for example. Or just use the knit stitch part on a stocking [stockinette] stitch edge, where extra elasticity is required. The instructions below are for a double rib, so for single rib just work one knit technique followed by one purl.

STEP 1: (Cast off knitwise).
Yarn round needle from right to left and back to right, going over then under needle.

STEP 2:
Knit the first st.

STEP 3:
Take 'st' created by yarn round needle over knitted st.

STEP 4:
Rep steps 1 to 3 for next knit st. Then take hold of first st left on RH needle and pass it over st just worked.

STEP 5: (Cast off purlwise).
Yarn round needle from right to left and back to right, going over then under needle

STEP 6:
Purl next st.

STEP 7:
Take 'st' created by yarn round needle over purled st.

STEP 8:
Take first st left on needle over second st. You will now only have one st on RH needle.
　Rep steps 5 to 8 for the next purl st.

Go back to Step 1 and repeat instructions for all sts across row, alternating the direction of yrn for knit and purl sts, as directed.

Grafting [Kitchener Stitch]

Although not used in any patterns in this book, grafting [Kitchener stitch] is such a handy technique that I thought I would include it for future reference. It is the process of joining two pieces of knitting together without a seam, so that the sewn stitches merge into the knitting. The example is done using stocking [stockinette] stitch as this is the most commonly used version.

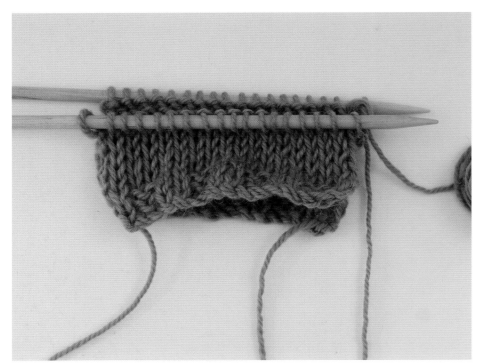

STEP 1:
Place two pieces to be grafted WS tog, with long length of yarn coming from back piece and tips of needle facing the same way. Thread a darning needle with the long length of yarn.

STEP 2:
Insert darning needle into first st pwise, leaving st on knitting needle.

STEP 3:
Insert darning needle into first st on back piece kwise, leaving st on knitting needle.

STEP 4:
Insert darning needle into first st on front knitting needle kwise, slipping it off knitting needle.

STEP 5:
Insert darning needle into next st on front needle pwise and pull yarn through, but leave st on knitting needle.

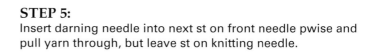

STEP 6:
Insert darning needle into first st on back needle pwise, slipping it off knitting needle.

STEP 7:
Insert darning needle into next st on back knititng needle kwise, leaving st on knitting needle, pulling yarn through.
    Repeat Steps 4–7.

I-Cord

I-cords are tubes created by knitting with two or three double pointed needles. The three needle method is a little more complex, so this tutorial will just teach the two needle method. This is a lovely, simple technique, which has several applications. It can be used to create handles (as in project 12) or an edging for a garment (as in project 16), or rolled up to create a placemat or coaster. The applications of this technique are only limited by the imagination of the user. What's more, it is as easy as pie. The simple rule is that you never need to turn your work. You transfer the knitting from one double pointed needle to another each time you knit a row, but do not ever turn the work round to the 'wrong side'. The most stitches you can use for your tube is six and only with thinner yarn and smaller needles. For thicker yarn and larger needles, three to four stitches are the maximum you can carry your yarn across.

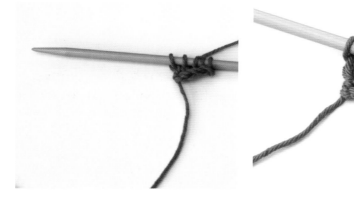

STEP 1:
Using dpns, cast on 5 sts and knit one row. Do not turn work.

STEP 2:
Slide the 5 sts to the other end of the dpn. Insert other dpn into first st, and carry yarn attached to ball across the back of work to start the next row. Knit the row. Rep Step 2.

You will never turn your work like this, but this photo shows what it will look like on the other side. See how the yarn carried across the back brings the two edges of the knitting together, with just a small gap between them where the yarn appears as a horizontal 'stitch'.

I-cord Edging

An alternative to a rib or garter stitch edging, the i-cord technique can be used to create a thin edging. Because it is double thickness and does not curl, it is very useful for edging stocking [stockinette] stitch garments where you want to keep the continuity of the stockinette appearance right to the edge. The tutorial shows two colours to emphasize the detail, but the edging can be done in the same colour as the main piece as in project 16. This tutorial is shown in 4 ply yarn using 3.75mm [US5] needles.

STEP 1:
Cast on 5 sts for i-cord edging. Knit one row. Do not move sts to other end of needle yet, you are going to join the i-cord to the knitting first.

STEP 2:
Insert dpn between first and second st of first row of the main knitted piece (with RS facing), as you would if picking up and knitting sts along the edge, and knit st.

STEP 3:
Pass fifth st from i-cord over top of st you picked up and knitted in previous step.

This is what your work will look like after Step 3.

STEP 4:
Move sts to over end of needle, carry yarn across back of i-cord and knit the next row.

I-cord Button Holes

Work as for i-cord above, but at place where button hole is required, work 2 rows of i-cord without joining to the main knitted piece omitting steps 2 and 3.

Rep steps 2–4 until end of work. Cast [bind] off.

At end of next row of i-cord, insert needle and knit stitch as in Step 2, missing out two rows of the main garment. This keeps the i-cord at the same tension as the main piece of knitting, whilst also creating a hole between it and the knitting which will be your buttonhole. Space buttonholes evenly up work by marking the position of buttonholes on the body of garment, and then missing out two rows of knitting each time you encounter a pin.

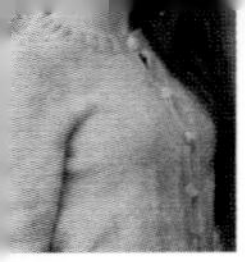

PROJECT 17: MISS WILMOTT

Woman's Cardi

The Bluefaced Leicester wool in this yarn softens it to make a comfortable, light and warm garment. This classic style cardigan will see you through many winters. Knit it up in a neutral colour to pair with more or less any other colour, or knit in a bright colour to make a statement. A trusty staple for a beginner to start their handknit wardrobe.

Materials
8 (9, 10, 11, 12, 13) x 50g balls (photographed in Fawn) Blacker Classic Lleyn Wool with 30% Bluefaced Leicester DK
Pair 3.75mm [US5] and 4mm [US6] ndls
3 stitch holders, or equivalent
8 buttons

TENSION
19 sts and 25 rows to 10cm [4in] square measured over stocking [stockinette] stitch using 4mm [US6] ndls.

Finished measurements
Width: 44.5 (45, 48, 49.5, 52.5, 54)cm [17¼ (17¾, 19, 19½, 20¾, 21¼)in]
Length: 66 (67, 68, 68, 69, 70)cm [26 (26¼, 26¾, 26¾, 27, 27½)in]
Sleeve seam: 44 (44.5, 45, 45, 46, 47)cm [17¼ (17½, 17¾, 17¾, 18, 18½]in)
Designed to fit with 5cm [2in] positive ease.

To fit
Size: 8 (10, 12, 14, 16, 18)
Chest: Chest 82 (86, 92, 97, 103, 107)cm [32 (34, 36, 38, 40, 42)in]

Abbreviations
See chart on page 127 for specific abbreviations.

How to make

Back
Cast on 82 (86, 90, 94, 98, 102) sts using Blacker Classic DK and 3.75mm [US5] ndls.
Work in rib patt as folls:
  Row 1: (K2, p2) rep to last 2 sts, k2.
  Row 2: (P2, k2) rep to last 2 sts, p2.
  Rep last 2 rows until you have worked 12 rows altogether in rib patt.
Change to 4mm [US6] ndls, and work in st st without shaping until work meas 39 (39.5, 40, 40, 40.5, 41)cm [15¼ (15½, 15¾, 15¾, 16, 16¼)in], ending with a WS row.

Shape Armholes
Cast [bind] off 4 sts at beg of next 2 rows. 74 (78, 82, 86, 90, 94) sts.
  Next row (RS): K2, k2tog, k to last 4 sts, skpo, k2. 72 (76, 80, 84, 88, 92) sts.
  Next row: P2, P2togtbl, p to last 4 sts, p2tog, p2. 70 (74, 78, 82, 86, 90) sts.
  Rep last 2 rows once more. 66 (70, 74, 78, 82, 86) sts.
Cont straight in st st without shaping until work meas 64 (65, 66, 67, 67, 68)cm [25 (25½, 26, 26¼, 26¼, 26¾)in], ending with a WS row.

Right shoulder
  Next row (RS): Cast [bind] off 4 sts, k13 (14, 15, 16, 17, 18) sts, turn and work on these 14 (15, 16, 17, 18, 19) sts only.
  Next row: Cast [bind] off 2 sts, p to end. 12 (13, 14, 15, 16, 17) sts
  Next row: Cast [bind] off 3 sts, k to last 2 sts, k2tog. 8 (9, 10, 11, 12, 13) sts

Next row: P2tog, p to end. 7 (8, 9, 10, 11, 12) sts

Cast [bind] off rem 7 (8, 9, 10, 11, 12) sts

Left shoulder

Place centre 30 (32, 34, 36, 38, 40) sts onto a holder, k to end.

   Next row: Cast [bind] off 4 sts, p to end. 14 (15, 16, 17, 18, 19) sts.

   Next row: Cast [bind] off 2 sts, k to end. 12 (13, 14, 15, 16, 17) sts.

   Next row: Cast [bind] off 3 sts, p to last 2 sts, p2tog. 8 (9, 10, 11, 12, 13) sts.

   Next row: K2tog, k to end. 7 (8, 9, 10, 11, 12) sts.

Cast [bind] off rem 7 (8, 9, 10, 11, 12) sts.

Right front

Cast on 42 (42, 46, 46, 50, 50) sts using 3.75mm [US5] ndls.

Work in rib patt as folls:

   Row 1 (RS): (K2, p2) rep to last 2 sts, k2.

   Row 2 (WS): (P2, k2) rep to last 2 sts, p2.

   Buttonhole row: K2, yrn, p2tog, (k2, p2) rep to last 2 sts, k2.

Cont in rib patt, starting from Row 2, and work a further 9 rows, making 12 rows of rib altogether, including buttonhole row.

Change to 4mm [US6] ndls*

   Work in st st patt with rib edge, as folls:

   Row 1 (RS): (K1, p1) 3 times, k to end.

   Row 2 (WS): P to last 6 sts, (k1, p1) 3 times.

Cont in patt as set without shaping, working buttonhole row on RS rows six more times at approx. 8 (8, 8.5, 8.5, 9, 9) cm [3 (3, 3¼, 3¼, 3½, 3½)in] intervals throughout Right Front instructions, measuring from first buttonhole to place second buttonhole, and so on. The buttonhole row you should work is as folls:

   Buttonhole row (RS): K1, p1, yrn, p2tog, k1, p1, k to end.

Cont in patt until work meas 39 (39.5, 40, 40, 40.5, 41)cm [15¼ (15½, 15¾, 15¾, 16, 16¼)in], ending with a RS row.

Shape Armhole

Cont in patt, cast [bind] off 4 sts at beg of next row. 38 (38, 42, 42, 46, 46) sts.

Work 1 row.

Next row (WS): P2, p2tog, patt to end. 37 (37, 41, 41, 45, 45) sts

Next row (RS): Patt to last 4 sts, k2tog, k2. 36 (36, 40, 40, 44, 44) sts

Rep last 2 rows once more. 34 (34, 38, 38, 42, 42) sts

Cont in patt without shaping until armhole meas 15 (15, 16, 16, 17, 17)cm [6 (6, 6¼, 6¼, 6¾, 6¾)in], ending with a WS row.

Shape Neck

Next Row (RS): Patt 6 sts, transfer these 6 sts to a length of contrasting yarn, k to end. 28 (28, 32, 32, 36, 36) sts

Next Row (WS): P to last 2 sts, p2tog. 27 (27, 31, 31, 35, 35) sts

Next Row: Cast [bind] off 3 sts, k to end. 24 (24, 28, 28, 32, 32) sts

Next Row: P to last 2 sts, p2tog. 23 (23, 27, 27, 31, 31) sts

Next Row: Cast [bind] off 2 sts, k to end. 21 (21, 25, 25, 29, 29) sts

Work in plain st st (the rib border is finished), dec one st at neck edge (beg of RS row) on next and every foll row until 14 (15, 16, 17, 18, 19) sts rem using p2tog on WS and k2tog on RS.

Cont without shaping until work meas 64 (65, 66, 67, 67, 68)cm [25 (25½, 26, 26¼, 26¼, 26¾)in],

ending with a RS row.

Right shoulder

Next row (WS): Cast [bind] off 4 sts, p to end. 10 (11, 12, 13, 14, 15) sts

Next row: K.

Next row: Cast [bind] off 3 sts, p to end. 7 (8, 9, 10, 11, 12) sts

Next row: K.

Cast [bind] off rem 7 (8, 9, 10, 11, 12) sts

Left front

Work as for Right Front until *, omitting buttonholes.

Work in st st patt with rib edge, as folls:

Row 1 (RS): K to last 6 sts, (p1, k1) 3 times.

Row 2 (WS): (P1, k1) 3 times, p to end.

Cont in patt as set without shaping until work meas 39 (39.5, 40, 40, 40.5, 41)cm [15¼ (15½, 15¾, 15¾, 16, 16¼)in], ending with a WS row.

Shape Armhole

Cont in patt, cast [bind] off 4 sts at beg of next row. 38 (38, 42, 42, 46, 46) sts.

Next Row (WS): (P1, k1) 3 times, p to end.

Next Row (RS): K2, k2tog, patt to end. 37 (37, 41, 41, 45, 45) sts

Next Row: Patt to last 4 sts, p2tog, p2. 36 (36, 40, 40, 44, 44) sts

Rep last 2 rows once more. 34 (34, 38, 38, 42, 42) sts

Cont in patt without shaping until armhole meas 15 (15, 16, 16, 17, 17)cm [6 (6, 6¼, 6¼, 6¾, 6¾)in], ending with a RS row.

Shape Neck

Next Row (WS): Patt 6 sts, transfer these 6 sts to a holder, p to end. 28 (28, 32, 32, 36, 36) sts

Next Row: K to last 2 sts, k2tog. 27 (27, 31, 31, 35, 35) sts

Next Row: Cast [bind] off 3 sts, p to end. 24 (24, 28, 28, 32, 32) sts

Next Row: K to last 2 sts, k2tog. 23 (23, 27, 26, 30, 30) sts

Next Row: Cast [bind] off 2 sts, p to end. 21 (21, 25, 25, 28, 28) sts

Work in plain st st (the rib border is finished), dec one st at neck edge (beg of WS row) on next WS and every foll row until 14 (15, 16, 17, 18, 19) sts rem.

Cont without shaping until work meas 64 (65, 66, 67, 67, 68)cm [25 (25½, 26, 26¼, 26¼, 26¾)in], ending with a WS row.

Left shoulder

Next row: Cast [bind] off 4 sts, k to end. 10 (11, 12, 13, 14, 15) sts.

Next row: P.

Next row: Cast [bind] off 3 sts, k to end. 7 (8, 9, 10, 11, 12) sts.

Next row: P.

Cast [bind] off rem 7 (8, 9, 10, 11, 12) sts.

Sleeves

Cast on 34 (34, 38, 38, 42, 42) sts using 3.75mm [US5] ndls.

Work in rib patt as folls:

Row 1 (RS): (K2, p2) to last 2 sts, k2.

Row 2 (WS): (P2, k2) to last 2 sts, p2.

Rep last 2 rows until you have worked 12 rows altogether in rib patt.

Change to 4mm [US6] ndls, and

work in st st, inc one st at each end of 3rd and every foll 6th row until 42 (54, 52, 64, 60, 70) sts and then on every foll 8th row to 56 (60, 62, 66, 68, 72) sts.

Cont in st st without shaping until work meas 44 (44.5, 45, 45, 46, 47)cm [17¼ (17½, 17¾, 17¾, 18, 18¼)in], ending with a WS row.

Shape Top of Sleeve

Cast [bind] off 4 sts at beg of next 2 rows. 48 (52, 54, 58, 60, 64) sts.

Next row (RS): K2, k2tog, k to last 4 sts, skpo, k2. 46 (50, 52, 56, 58, 62) sts.

Next row: P2, P2togtbl, p to last 4 sts, p2tog, p2. 44 (48, 50, 54, 56, 60) sts.

Rep last 2 rows once more. 40 (44, 46, 50, 52, 56) sts.

Work four rows in st st without shaping.

Cont in st st, dec one st at each end of next (RS) and every foll 4th row, 2 sts in from edge, as above, until 30 (34, 36, 40, 42, 44) sts rem, then on every RS row until 22 (24, 28, 30, 34, 36) sts rem, then on every row until 12 (16, 18, 22, 24, 26) sts rem.

Sizes 8 (10, 12) only

Cast [bind] off rem sts.

Sizes 14 (16, 18) only

Cast [bind] off 4 sts at beg of next 2 rows. 14 (16, 18) sts.

Cast [bind] off rem sts.

Neck Border

Join both shoulder seams using back stitch (page 63).

Neck border is knitted using your larger size ndl because it is a relaxed neckline.

Using 4mm [US 6] ndls, and with RS facing, (k1, p1) three times across sts from Right Front holder, pick up and knit 17 (15, 19, 18, 22, 20) sts up shaped section of Right Front neck, then 9 (10, 7, 9, 6, 7) sts up straight edge of Right Front to shoulder, pick up and knit 4 sts down shaped section of right back neck, then knit 30 (32, 34, 36, 38, 40) sts from holder, pick up and knit 4 sts up shaped section of left back neck, then pick up and knit 9 (10, 7, 9, 6, 7) sts down straight section of Left Front neck, and 17 (15, 19, 18, 22, 20) sts down shaped section of Left Front neck, (p1, k1) three times across sts from left front holder. 102 (102, 106, 110, 114, 114) sts.

Work in patt as folls:

Row 1 (WS): (P1, k1) three times, (p2, k2) to last 8 sts, p2, (k1, p1) three times.

Row 2: (K1, p1) three times, (k2, p2) to last 8 sts, k2, (p1, k1) three times.

Row 3: As Row 1.

Row 4 (buttonhole row): K1, p1, yrn, p2tog, k1, p1, (k2, p2) to last 8 sts, k2, (p1, k1) three times.

Row 5: As Row 1.

Rep Rows 2 and 3 once more.

Cast [bind] off in rib.

Making Up

Mark centre position of sleeves at cast off edge with a pin. With RS tog, pin sleeves to sleeve edge of fronts and back, making sure marker is in line with shoulder seam, and easing sleeves into armholes if necessary to fit. Once you have an even fit, sew sleeves to front and back using back stitch. With RS facing, sew up sleeve seams and side seams using mattress stitch (page 62), taking care to match up rows, and rib cuffs. Sew in ends, taking any ends that are close to cuffs up the seams inside (see page 60), rather than along rows close to the cast on/cast off edges. Sew buttons on to button band (left front), making sure they are spaced at same intervals as buttonholes.

PROJECT 18: TOMMY

Man's Tank Top

A vintage style tank top in a fine yet warm yarn, designed in a plain and simple style to go with anything. Looks great with a plain or patterned shirt, or under a jacket. There are several colours in the Libby Summers Fine Aran range which would be suitable for this garment, which is an essential for any stylish man's wardrobe.

Materials
6 (7, 8, 9) x 50g balls Libby Summers Fine Aran (photographed in 874 Vintage Green)
Pair 4mm [US6] ndls
Pair 5mm [US7] ndls
Circular 4mm [US6] ndl for neckband
Stitch holder
Stitch marker
Darning ndl for sewing up

How to make
Back

Cast on 85 (89, 93, 97) sts using Libby Summers Fine Aran and 4mm [US6] ndls.

Work 14 rows in Rib Patt as folls:

Row 1 (RS): (K1, p1) rep to last st, k1.

Row 2 (WS): (P1, k1) rep to last st, p1.

Change to 5mm [US7] ndls and beg with a k row, work in st st, inc 1 st at both ends of 3rd, and next foll 8th (8th, 10th, 10th) row to 89 (93, 97, 101) sts and then on every foll 12th row to 93 (97, 101, 105) sts.

Cont straight until work meas 42 (43, 44, 45)cm [16½ (17, 17¼, 17¾)in].

Shape Armholes
Cast [bind] off 7 sts at beg of next 2 rows. 79 (83, 87, 91) sts.

TENSION
18 sts and 24 rows to 10cm/4in measured over st st on 5mm [US7] ndls

Finished Measurements
Width underarms: 51.5 (54, 56, 58.5)cm/20¼ (21¼, 22, 23)in
Length from base of neckline to hemline: 67 (69, 71, 73)cm/26 (27, 28, 28¾)in
Designed to fit with 6.5cm/2½in positive ease
To adjust length of garment, work extra length or less length before armhole shaping, depending on fit required.

To fit
Chest 97.5 (102, 107, 112)cm/38 (40, 42, 44)in

Abbreviations
See chart p. 127 for specific abbreviations.

Dec 1 st at both ends of next 2 rows and next alt row. 73 (77, 81, 85) sts*.

Cont straight until armhole meas 25 (26, 27, 28)cm [10 (10¼, 10¾, 11)in] from **Shape Armholes**, ending with a WS row.

Shape Shoulder
Cast [bind] off 8 (8, 8, 9) sts at beg of next 4 rows. 41 (45, 49, 49) sts.

Cast [bind] off 6 (6, 7, 7) sts at beg of next 2 rows. 29 (33, 35, 35) sts.

Leave rem sts on a holder.

Front
Work as for Back to *.

Cont straight until work meas 49 (52, 53, 54)cm [19¼ (20½, 21, 21¼)in] from cast on edge ending on a WS row.

Divide for neck
Next row (RS): K35 (37, 39, 41), skpo. Turn and work on these 36 (38, 40, 42) sts only as folls:

Next row (WS): Purl.

Next row: K to last 2 sts, skpo. 35 (37, 39, 41) sts.

Rep last 2 rows until you have 22 (22, 23, 25) sts.

Cont straight until work meas same as Back to shoulder shaping, ending with WS row.

Cont in st st, cast [bind] off 8 (8, 8, 9) sts at beg of next and foll alt row. 6 (6, 7, 7) sts.

Cast [bind] off 6 (6, 7, 7) sts at beg of next row.

With RS facing, rejoin yarn to rem 36 (38, 40, 42) sts.

Next row (RS): K2tog, k to end. 35 (37, 39, 41) sts.

Next row (WS): Purl.

Rep last 2 rows until you have 22 (22, 23, 25) sts, ending with WS facing for next row.

Cont in st st, cast [bind] off 8 (8, 8, 9) sts at beg of next and foll

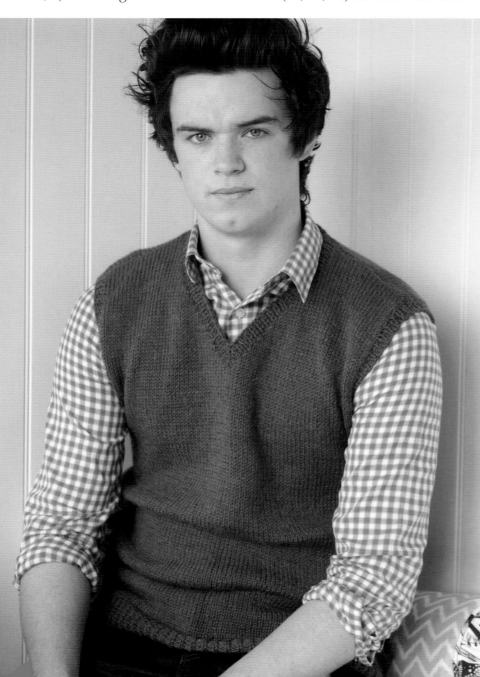

alt row. 6 (6, 7, 7) sts.

Cast [bind] off 6 (6, 7, 7) sts at beg of next row.

Making up
Neckband
With RS tog join left shoulder seam using back stitch.

With RS facing and using 4mm [US6] circular ndl, knit across 29 (33, 35, 35) sts left on a holder from back neck, pick up and knit 44 (46, 46, 48) sts down left side

neck, place a marker on ndl (see p. 122–3) , pick up and knit 44 (46, 46, 48) sts up right side of neck. 117 (125, 127, 131) sts.

Row 1 (WS): Beg with p1, work in k1, p1 rib over first 44 (46, 46, 48) sts (ending with k1), slip marker to RH ndl, beg with k1, work in k1, p1 rib to end of row.

Row 2: Rib as set to 2 sts before marker, skpo, sl marker to RH ndl, k2tog, rib to end.

Row 3: Rib as set to 2 sts before marker, p2tog, sl marker to RH ndl, p2togtbl, rib to end.

Rep rows 2 and 3 once (once, twice, twice) more.

Cast [bind] off on RS using rib method.

With RS tog join right shoulder seam using back stitch.

Armhole edges
With RS facing and using 4mm [US6] circular ndl, pick up and knit 43 (44, 46, 48) sts from right back armhole, and 44 (45, 47, 49) sts from right front armhole, making sure you start and finish right at the edge of work (this means picking up from the few sts cast off for armholes, as well as up the side of work). 87 (89, 93, 97) sts.

Work 4 rows in rib patt as given for Back.

Cast [bind] off.

Repeat Armhole edge instructions, picking up sts first from left front armhole and then left back armhole for the other side.

Sew up side seams with RS facing, using mattress stitch.

KEEPING TRACK AND MAKING THE GRADE

The patterns in this book are essentially progressive, taking you through from the simplest straight garter stitch project with no sewing up, to making your own fully sleeved garment, and all stages in between. Where more complex stitch patterns are tackled, a simpler shaped or smaller sized project is used, and where more complex shaped or sized projects are tackled, such as the cardigans and tank top, then the projects use the simpler stocking stitch pattern. Bear these principles in mind when choosing further projects and keep at least one element of the design simple. Even with carefully chosen projects, you will undoubtedly encounter problems and make mistakes – this is an inevitable process of learning a new skill. Here are a few tips to help with frustration, doubt, mistakes and dilemmas.

Keeping track of your progress and following the pattern

The most common mistakes knitters make can be easily avoided with a bit of preparation and monitoring. Many knitters plunge straight into the cast on row in their eagerness to start a new project, but a little patience will save much heartache. So before you start, make sure you do the following:

1. Study the materials, abbreviations, measurements and tension and make sure you have calculated what size you want to make (if there is a choice).

2. Check your tension, that you have enough of the right yarn, the correct needles and other materials for your project.

3. Read through the instructions. Don't worry if you cannot really follow what's going on at this stage. Knitting instructions can be difficult to properly understand unless you are doing the actual work. The most important thing is to make sure that you theoretically understand the construction of the project – how many pieces it has, what direction they are knitted in (e.g. bottom up, top down), if there is shaping and whether it is clear from the picture where it starts and finishes. Look for changes in texture and colour, and where they occur. These pointers will help ensure that you do not omit rows or knit too much.

4. Mark the pattern. You don't want to spoil your pattern or book, so photocopy the bit you are working on first. Highlight the size you are working, tick off rows worked and make notes in the margins to help you keep track of your progress. If the pattern requires you to work '20 rows in st st....' for example, then keep a tally in the margins. Always double check this against your actual knitting when you think you've knitted 20 rows. You might have been distracted and forgotten to mark a couple of rows. It is always better to be safe than sorry. Don't be impatient. Knitting is wonderful for teaching patience and delayed gratification.

5. Record any changes you make to the pattern for whatever reason whether it is because the pattern has a mistake in it (which does sometimes happen) or because you decided on a variation. This is particularly important if making a garment or if the project has more than one piece because you will need to adjust the other pieces as well. Never assume that you will remember what you have done later on. Working it out by peering at your knitting under a microscope will probably not help either, particularly if you are trying to work out what you did after sewing up, because the stitches that have been incorporated into the seam will conceal what actually happened.

6. Monitor your progress as you are going along. Don't just blindly follow the pattern without thinking what you are doing, and without looking at your work. This might sound obvious, but knitting is a rhythmic and almost meditative activity which can mean entering a kind of reverie which takes over your mind and the fact that you are actually following quite specific instructions can be forgotten. I am not suggesting that you don't allow yourself to enjoy and relax while working but if knitting a complicated pattern, you will need to concentrate and even with a simple pattern you will need to program your brain. If you are a beginner, make sure you allow yourself plenty of experience of knitting simple patterns before progressing. You do not want to put yourself off by getting frustrated with patterns which are beyond your current capabilities.

Measuring

Bear in mind that stitches are always wider than they are tall. Your knitting is elastic. If you stretch it width-ways while measuring the length, the measurement will be shorter than it should be. If you stretch it lengthways while measuring the width, the measurement will be smaller than it should be. Always lie your knitting absolutely flat and do not be tempted to pull it around. By all means smooth over any crinkles and creases but other than that the stitches will lie in their natural state and this is how the work should be measured.

Three principles for measuring:

1. Measure at least 2.5cm [1in] in from ribbings, gatherings and edgings. This applies both ways.

2. When a pattern requires you to make two pieces of an identical length, don't use a tape measure for the second piece, instead count the rows you worked for the first piece and then replicate that number.

3. Counting stitches/rows on the right side is easy when you understand that the knit stitch is a complete 'V'. The boundaries of a purl stitch are less defined, looking something like a sine wave ⌒⌒, joining up with each other across the row to create a series of waves. When counting rows on a purl side, count the top of each wave as a row.

Lifelines

I was taught to knit by my mother and grandmother and they never used lifelines so neither did I, but I gather that a lot of knitters do. Lifelines are used in two ways. Firstly, to pre-empt possible mistakes. Insert a lifeline at the row you have reached, knowing that your previous rows are correct and that the rows you are about to tackle are tricky and might need unravelling. Thread a darning needle with a length of contrasting yarn which is thinner than the yarn you are using and about twice the width of your knitting, then thread the yarn through all stitches on the needle. Work the row as normal, making sure you do not knit more loosely as a result of the lifeline. If you go wrong in the next section, you can pull the knitting off the needles with confidence, knowing that your work will not unravel beyond the position of the lifeline.

The second way of using a lifeline is just before unravelling your knitting, after having noticed a mistake. This method is a little more tricky and I have included a tutorial for it in the next section.

CORRECTING MISTAKES

It would be impossible to cover every type of mistake in this book so we will just look at three common mistakes and how to correct them.

1. Missing rows or extra rows

If you find you have knitted too many rows, or missed out some rows and need to take work back to the point before this, unravel your knitting stitch by stitch or pull the needles out and unravel whole rows, before placing stitches back on needle (use lifelines if necessary). If following the second method, take care to place the stitches on the needle the right way round, and all facing the same way. Also, count the stitches when you have them all safely on the needle to check you have not dropped any. The following tutorial shows how to place a lifeline and unravel back to this point.

STEP 1:
Thread your darning needle with a length of contrasting yarn. Insert needle through right hand side of first st of row you wish to mark and pull through. Making sure you stay on the same horizontal row, thread yarn through all sts across the row.

STEP 2:
Remove needles from sts and placing knitting on a flat surface, start unravelling rows by tugging yarn gently.

STEP 3:
Unravel back to the lifeline. You know you have got there when the contrasting yarn is holding the stitches as the knitting needle would.

STEP 4:
Starting from the side of the knitting furthest from the yarn attached to the ball, insert knitting needle into the stitches held by the lifeline one by one, taking care to put them all on the needle facing the same direction.

2. One-stitch errors

If you have made a mistake on just one stitch in the current row, undo the row stitch by stitch up to the point the error occurred and redo the stitches. If the error occurred one or more rows below the current row, undo the row you are working on stitch by stitch to the vertical point in the knitting where the error occurred and then unravel that one stitch down to the row where the error occurred. Correct the error and then pick up the stitch using a crochet hook, and bring it back to the current row one by one by hooking it over each of the horizontal loops of yarn which are hanging loose behind it. This is easier to carry out on the right side of work.

STEP 1:
If you notice a dropped or erroneous st, unpick to the st before the problem as follows. Insert LH needle into loop below st on needle.

STEP 2:
Slip st off RH needle, and at same time keep loop picked up with LH needle on LH needle. Gently tug yarn to undo st from current row.
   Repeat STEP 1–2 until you get to the problem area.

STEP 3:
Pick up dropped or erroneous st with crochet hook.

STEP 4:
If the stitch needs altering, do so using the crochet hook. If it needs to be taken up some rows to the current row, hook it over the loose loops at the back of the dropped st, one at a time, starting with the lowest, and bring it to the same level as the sts on your LH needle.

STEP 5:
Pass the picked up st onto the LH needle and it is ready to be re-worked.

3. Correcting Uneven Stitches

Sometimes your tension can go awry just over one or two stitches, usually because of a lapse in concentration. The stitch might be too baggy or too tight. If the uneven stitch is on the current row, unravel back to the uneven stitch and work again. If the uneven stitch is on a previous row, you might get away with not unravelling to that row, particularly if the stitch is close to the edge and you are working on straight needles.

If you are working on straight needles and the uneven stitch is close to the edge of work, correct the tension in the stitch by gently pulling it with the tip of a spare needle, or the stitches next to it (if it is too loose). In the case of stitches that are too loose, you can carry the extra looseness to the edge of the work, and then conceal it when sewing up. If the work is not going to have a seam, you cannot do this and will need to unravel the rows.

If you are working in the round, it may be more difficult to conceal the unevenness because you will have to spread the unevenness out to the stitches on both sides. Use a spare needle to gently tease the stitch into shape. This will affect the stitches next to it, so you will need to do some remedial work on them as well. The result might not be satisfactory, in which case, you will have to unravel the rows, but it is worth a try first.

If the stitch is only slightly uneven, it is best to leave it alone and allow the blocking process to correct it. You can improve even badly uneven stitches a little during the blocking process. Block first, then examine the stitch to see if this has made a difference. If not, try and tease the stitch with a knitting needle to spread the unevenness out amongst the surrounding stitches. Then block work again.

The photo tutorial below shows how to correct a baggy stitch.

STEP 1:
Identify the baggy stitch.

STEP 2:
Insert spare needle into the side of the loop below which is nearest to the edge of work. Tug gently to tighten the stitch. Notice that the next st along will get more baggy in response.

STEP 3:
Repeat the same action with this st and so on all the way to the edge of work.

STEP 4:
Corrected stitches. The remaining unevenness can be corrected during blocking.

SIZING AND GRADING

Choosing the right project and getting the right fit

Considerations

Size – your measurements, the garment's finished measurements, fit
Practical – warmth, thickness, handle, cleaning, durability
Aesthetic – colour, texture, fit, fashion value
Cost – price of materials, cost in relation to lifespan
Personal – allergies, sensitivities, preferences, figure, fit

In order to choose the right project, you need to have an idea of what it is that you want. The list of considerations above should help you think things through before you buy a pattern and materials. Stylistic, practical and aesthetic considerations are the easiest to think through beforehand but perhaps more difficult, and sometimes overlooked, is the fit factor. Do you want your garment to be loose fitting, tight fitting or an exact fit? The differential between the 'Actual Chest Size' given in the pattern and the 'Finished Measurements' tells you what fit the design will give you.

Positive ease is a term used to describe the difference between your actual measurements and the finished measurements of the garment when the garment is bigger. If a garment has positive ease it will be loose fitting. How much positive ease will determine just how loose. So for example, a garment with 2.5cm [1in] positive ease will be fairly fitted, but one with 10cm [4in] will be loose fitting.

Negative ease is a term used to describe the difference between your actual measurements and the finished measurements of the garment when the garment is smaller. If a garment has negative ease, it will be tightly fitting.

Remember that yarn is naturally stretchy which is why you can knit something that is smaller than your size and still get it on. When choosing which size to knit, look at the photograph of the finished garment and decide if you want the same look. The model should be wearing the right size for his/her measurements. Look at the information at the top of the pattern about the size and actual measurements. Not all patterns have information about positive or negative ease and sometimes you will have to work this out yourself by comparing the actual measurements with the finished measurements for the same size. Where choosing a size becomes more difficult is when a pattern does not provide one or the other of these. Most do, but where they don't, the fit has been decided by the designer and you will be relying on the picture to decide if this is what you want.

Length and sleeve length

It is easier to adjust the length of a garment than it is the width, so it is important to decide on the correct chest size first. If you want a longer garment find the most appropriate place in the pattern to add extra rows. This should be before the armholes. If extra sleeve length is required, add this after any increases and before shaping the top.

Garment Styles and Features

The different features that make up a garment and styles within these features are too numerous to cover comprehensively in this book. However, it is useful for a new knitter to be aware of what features to look at when choosing a project, and consider the wide range of styles that these features might have. The table below gives some common styles and relates these to the knitting techniques which will probably be required. Note that this may vary depending on the direction of work and methods used.

Feature	Style	Techniques
Body	Straight	No shaping
	Tapered	Decrease or increase
	Inverted Tapered	Increase or decrease
	Mixed	Both increase and decrease techniques
Sleeves	Straight	No shaping
	Tapered	Decrease or increase
	Inverted Tapered	Increase or decrease
	Mixed	Both increase and decrease
Neckline	Round	Casting off and decrease techniques
	U shaped	Picking up stitches
	Scoop	Any technique
	V shaped	Decrease
Yokes	Round	Casting off and decrease techniques
	Square	Picking up stitches
	Tapered	Casting off
	Plunging	Decrease
Shoulders	Raglan	Decrease (increase if working top down)
	Set-in	Casting off and decrease
	Drop	No shaping
	Batwing	Decrease (increase if working top down)
	Saddle Shoulder	Casting off and decrease
Openings	Wide	No shaping usually
	Edge-to-edge	Decrease
	Overlapping	No shaping if straight (decrease if sloped)
	Wrap-over	Increase (decrease if working top down)
Cuffs	Ribbed cuffs	Alternating knit and purl sts
	Drawstring	Sudden increase across whole row
	Flat-stitched	Combinations of knit and purl/garter st
	Ruffle	Decrease and increase
Pockets	Patch (applied or picked up)	Sewing or picking up sts
	Slit (horizontal, sloping or vertical)	Casting off, casting on, increase/decrease
	Kangaroo	

Tapered, set in sleeve

Raglan sleeve

Drop shoulder, puff cuff sleeve

Straight body and sleeves with no shaping or neckline

Fitted waist with round yoke

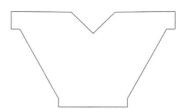

Batwing, (inverted taper) 'V' neck

Tapered with scoop neck, tapered sleeve and patch pocket

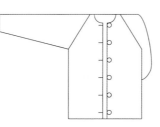

Button through, straight fit, tapered sleeve raglan cardigan

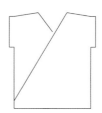

Sleeveless wrapover

Saddle shoulder

Abbreviations	Definition
alt	alternate
approx	approximately
beg	beginning
cm	centimetres
cn	cable needle
cont	continue
dec	decrease
foll	follows
in	inches
inc	increase
k	knit
k2tog	knit 2 sts together
k3tog	knit 3 stitches together, thus loosing 2 stitches from row
kfb	Knit into front loop of stitch and without slipping stitch off needle, knit into the back loop, then slip loop off needle, creating one extra stitch on RH needle
kfbf	Knit into front loop of stitch and without slipping stitch off needle, knit into the back loop without slipping stitch off needle, then knit into front of loop again, then slip loop off needle, creating two extra stitches on RH needle
kwise	knitwise
LH/RH	left hand/right hand
M1	pick up loop before next st and place on LH ndl, knit into back of loop, thus making one extra st
Make bobble	(k1, p1, k1) into next st, turn work, (k1, p1) into next 2 sts, turn, leaving 3rd st on LH ndl, once turned, sl left over st from RH ndl to LH ndl, and pass 4 sts over, sl st onto RH ndl
meas	measures
ndl(s)	needles
p	purl
patt	pattern
pfb	purl into front loop of stitch and without slipping off needle, knit into the back loop, then slip loop off needle, creating one extra stitch on RH needle.
pwise	purlwise
rem	remaining
rep	repeat
rnd	round (used with circular needles where knitting is worked continuously without being turned)
RS	right side
skpo	slip one st, knit one st, pass slipped st over top of knitted st
sl	slip
sl st	slip stitch
sl1	slip one stitch
sl3	slip 3 stitches
sppo	slip one st, purl one st, pass slipped st over top of purled st
st st	stocking stitch - knit on RS, purl on WS
st(s)	stitches
tbl	through back of loop
Wrap st on RS	Having just turned work onto RS, wrap st as folls: ensuring yarn is at back, slip first st from RH ndl to LH ndl, bring yarn to front, slip st back onto RH ndl. Take yarn to back to k next st.
Wrap st on WS	Having just turned work onto WS, wrap st as folls: ensuring yarn is at back, slip first st from RH ndl to LH ndl, bring yarn to front, slip st back onto RH ndl. Yarn is now ready to purl next st.
WS	wrong side
yb	yarn back
yf	yarn forward
yrn (yo)	yarn round needle (yarn over needle)

ACKNOWLEDGEMENTS

This book would not have been possible without the support and contribution of others

My amazing Mum, Carol Summers, for being my best and harshest critic, and most loyal supporter and helper. Thank you for checking all my patterns religiously, knitting frantically for me when required, and for your patience in teaching me to knit when I was knee high to a grasshopper all those years ago.

My fabulous Dad, Alastair Summers and my wonderful husband Matthew Redhead, for doing all those extra school runs and much more to give me the time I needed to write.

To my three precious girls for interrupting me less than usual, asking me how its going and showing an interest. You're all amazing.

To my sister and her husband for the use of your home to write and take photos.

Claire Rickett, for your invaluable ideas, in particular for helping me see things from the point of view of the less experienced knitter, for trying out patterns and for being cheerful at all times.

Rachel Vowles, my lovely tech editor, for your patience and meticulous editing.

Stephanie Boardman and Carol Summers for your superb pattern checking.

Don Lambert, for the great photos for the tutorials, for your patience with me, your willingness to stand in awkward positions to get the best shots, and for delivering the photos in record time.

Erin Franklin, Josh Tinton and Emily Morris for being fantastic and patient models.

My loyal team of brilliant knitters, Christina Guays-Atkins, Sarah Holmes, Jean Molloy, Jayne Fishenden, Pauline Scales, Carolyn Mellowes, Claire Rickett and Carol Summers. You all knitted cheerfully and patiently, and every single one of you delivered impeccable knitting bang on time.

Holly Willsher and Tessa Rose, my perfect and unflappable editors, giving the most efficient, precise and prompt replies to emails and phone calls I have ever come across in my professional life. It has been a pleasure to work for you from start to finish.

Easton Walled Gardens, for the use of their incredible gardens and romantic buildings for the photo shoot, providing the perfect backdrop to show off the projects.

Photography shot on Location by Libby Summers at Easton Walled Gardens, Easton, Grantham, Lincolnshire NG33 5AP Tel: 01476 530063 Fax: 01476 530063 Email: info@eastonwalledgardens.co.uk Website: www.eastonwalledgardens.co.uk

STOCKISTS

Projects	Specific Yarn used	Yarn company	Website	Telephone
1, 3, 8	Libby Summers Chunky	Libby Summers Ltd	www.libbysummers.co.uk	+44 7818286538
2, 5, 6, 14 15, 18	Libby Summers Fine Aran	Libby Summers Ltd	www.libbysummers.co.uk	+44 7818286539
4, 7	Artesano Aran	Artesano Yarns Ltd	www.artesanoyarns.co.uk	+44(0)118 9503350
9	Fyberspates Scrumptious DK Worsted	Fyberspates Luxury Yarns	www.fyberspates.co.uk	+44 (0)1829 732525
10	Sirdar Knit and Crochet Cotton DK	Sirdar Yarns	www.sirdar.co.uk	+44(0)1924 231 682
11	Fyberspates Vivacious DK	Fyberspates Luxury Yarns	www.fyberspates.co.uk	+44 (0)1829 732525
12	Rowan Cotton Glace, Rowan DK Handknit Cotton	Rowan Yarns	www.knitrowan.com	+44 (0)1484 681881
13	Manos Silk Blend DK	Manos Del Uruguay	www.manos.com.uy www.artesanoyarns.co.uk	+44(0)118 9503350
16	Sublime Extra Fine Merino DK	Sirdar Yarns	www.sirdar.co.uk	+44(0)1924 231 682
17	Blacker Classic Lleyn Wool with 30% Blue-faced Leicester DK	Blacker Yarns	www.blackeryarns.co.uk	+44 (0)1566 777 635